Jamaica's "Forgotten Prime Minister"
Donald Sangster

By Hartley Neita

PROUDLY
CELEBRATING
JAMAICA

Power is like fire—a good servant but a bad master, and the misuse of power is one of the greatest faults of any Government; indeed it is a crime against the people.

Donald Sangster

From an article in *The Voice* (July 27, 1957)

ACKNOWLEDGEMENTS

Michelle Anderson, Lee Binns, Madge Broderick, Karen Chambers, George Davis, Edley Deans, Patricia Dewar, Timothy Dewar-Neita, Prof. Neville Duncan, Derek Dyer, Anthony Falloon, Joyce Francis, Caswell Green, Mrs. Gunning, Mike Jarrett, Vin Kelly, Rev. Marjorie Lewis, Rupert Lewis, Samuel Lewis, Pauline Mason, Maxine McDonnough, Clovis McKnight, Joseph McPherson, Ambassador Don Mills, Elombe Mottley, Gary Neita, Gregory Neita, Karen Neita, Ken Parchment, Most Hon. P.J. Patterson, Lilla Patrick, Ryan Peralto, G.A. 'Buddy' Pouyat, Muriel 'Cissy' Pouyat, Sheree Rhoden, Earl Richards, Hon. Joyce Robinson, Lena Rose, Alicia Sangster, Doris Sangster, Bindley Sangster, Derrick Sangster, Kingsley Sangster, Velma Sangster, Judith Silvera, Jean Smith, Stephen Thompson, Michelle Welsh.

Very special thanks:
Dr the Hon. Alfred Sangster for his support and cooperation; Dr Donna Hope, PhD, MPhil, B.A., head of the research team; Tanya Francis, Daphne Clarke and Tanya Lawrence, researchers; Lance Neita, for his research into the early life of Donald Sangster; Troy Caine, political historian; Olive Senior, for contributing the foreword, and her support in the editorial process.

Michelle Neita, Editor.

CHASE Fund Ltd., for providing financial assistance to research, write and edit the manuscript, as well as to publish and launch the book.

Reference Sources
The Gleaner Library
Jamaica Information Service
Munro College Library
National Library of Jamaica
Public Opinion newspaper
The Voice newspaper

Printed in the United States of America

www.hartleyneitabooks.com

First Printing, 2012

ISBN 978-0-9829630-2-9

Minna Press
204 Mountain View Avenue
Kingston 6
Jamaica, W.I.

www.minnapress.com

Cover Design by Michelle Welsh
Design Associate Mark Steven Weinberger

CONTENTS

FOREWORD

Hartley Neita's book should be required reading as we celebrate Jamaica's 50th anniversary because it takes us back in an intimate way to the beginning, to that generation that crafted the new nation in 1962. The author himself was a witness to many of the momentous events which he describes. His book is easy to read, honest, entertaining and informative. Above all, it restores Donald Sangster to his rightful place in the pantheon of Jamaican leaders and provides the context for a better understanding of his life and his times.

The reader might be surprised to discover that while the quiet Sangster played second fiddle to the powerful Bustamante, he was in fact the real driver of Jamaica's economic and social development long before his untimely death.

Calling Donald Sangster 'The forgotten prime minister' is somewhat ironic since he held that office for only seven weeks; the last three weeks spent in a coma in a Montreal hospital where he died. What this book elaborates and what we should celebrate is Sangster's unstinting years of service to the nation starting with his election to the St Elizabeth Parochial Board when he was only 21, and lasting until his death in office at the age of 56.

Our failure, then, is not only to honour Sangster the prime minister but to honour Sangster the man who served his country so long and so well. The failure to mark the centenary of his birth on 26 October 2011 is symptomatic of an attitude over the years to ignore the existence of Donald Sangster so that he remains a vague name to younger generations.

Oblivion might be due to our short memories and our tendency to ignore the past and concentrate on the more ephemeral aspects of our heritage. But, his death was also marked by controversy and rumours that persist to this day. Neita does deal with this issue, setting forth the facts in the form of the medical details surrounding Sangster's illness and final days. He fell ill shortly after being sworn in as prime minister and while he was at work crafting a new budget in his capacity as finance minister.

Some of the oversight might also be due to the fact that Sangster's tenure in politics coincided with the rise and leadership of the two giants that everyone knows about—Norman Washington Manley and William Alexander Bustamante—and that he served most of his time in the shadow of the latter who reigned as undisputed leader of the Jamaica Labour Party (JLP).

Yet, as this book demonstrates, Sangster can also be seen as the pivot around which much of Jamaica's growth in stature from colony to nation turned in the years immediately before and after Independence. He was always in Bustamante's shadow yet Bustamante thrust him into the limelight. As a member of Bustamante's inner circle, in office or out, he was a trusted JLP standard-bearer from 1949, first as first deputy leader, later deputy prime minister and then acting prime minister. He also held the important ministerial portfolio of finance in successive JLP governments from 1953. Internationally, he was recognised as a respected leader and negotiator, at a time when The Commonwealth was a meaningful concept. His skilful diplomacy and interventions won international respect for Jamaica.

His training as a lawyer and accountant, and his diplomatic skills, made him an active figure in the negotiations leading to the ill-fated West Indies Federation, and then in Jamaica's negotiations with Whitehall to go it alone. As chairman of the committee that organised the Independence celebrations, he played a central role in the choices made in regard to Jamaica's National Flag, Anthem and other National Symbols.

In 1967 Sangster led the JLP to an election victory, the first time that Bustamante—finally admitting incapacity —did not lead the campaign. The *Gleaner's* commentary at the time throws into relief the crucial Bustamante-Sangster relationship:

> Sir Alexander Bustamante is a great leader but—as everyone knows – he is temperamental. Obedience to him which has always been Mr Sangster's dedication is no easy role. Yet between the sometimes tempestuous Busta and the frequently apologetic Donald, there was always a nexus of political and personal affinity which has proved stronger than all the other relationships among the vigorous contentions inside the Jamaica Labour Party.

Whereas Ministers of rash and radical mien with lively street corner vigour seemed to be more in harmony with the charismatic leadership of Sir Alexander, the quiet administrative thoroughness of Mr Sangster made him almost indispensable in transforming an emotional labour movement into a workable parliamentary party and government.

Sangster certainly seemed to have understood Bustamante better than most of his colleagues. Or, perhaps, he simply had a stronger sense of his own worth. The following observation by Hartley Neita tells us much about Sangster's discipline and self-restraint under Bustamante: "He was in the position of the captain of an aircraft who was likely to have the controls wrenched out of his hands at any moment. Yet, he bore this paradoxical situation without complaint."

Without being given further analysis of Sangster's personality, we can only make certain assumptions, one of which could be that his privileged yet disciplined rural background provided him with the stability and self-assurance that enabled him to quietly ride the waves of political upheavals.

As Neita points out, Sangster was a wealthy young man, handsome, polished and bright, and had no need to enter public life. But serve he did, inspired perhaps by the example of his uncle, a member of the Legislative Council, for whom he campaigned at age 16 while still at Munro College. Or, perhaps, he had from the start the burning ambition of the country boy to make something of himself that would transcend the borders of his inheritance. That we do not know, because we are not made privy to his thoughts or inner life. What we have is Neita's external presentation of Sangster as a well-rounded individual—a man who was Christian and abstemious in his habits yet nevertheless enjoyed life. He loved theatre, good food, dancing, sports and seems to have had a wide circle of friends. He comes across as compassionate and generous and involved himself in the life of his parish of birth—St Elizabeth and that of his later political representation—North East Clarendon.

In this book he is portrayed as untouched by scandal —a golden boy from birth, which makes the story of his end and the death-watch that accompanied his weeks of coma unbearably sad. He was knighted by Queen Elizabeth while on his deathbed, so he never enjoyed that honour and it is hard, even now, to think of him as 'Sir Donald'.

Sangster was never one to blow his own trumpet, and in Hartley Neita he acquired a biographer as subtle as he was. Neita occupied the sensitive position of press officer or press secretary to five heads of government – Norman Manley, Bustamante, Sangster, Shearer, and Michael Manley—which means that he was privy to state secrets and witnessed some of the most intimate moments in our modern political history. The fact that both parties put such trust in him speaks of his ability and trustworthiness. He died in 2008, having completed a first draft of this book; the task of editing it and seeing it to fruition has been ably carried out by his daughter, Michelle Neita.

But even though he was writing this biography in the age of disclosure, the age of Facebook, Twitter and whistleblowing, Hartley Neita still maintained the posture of discreet public servant, setting forth the facts about Donald Sangster's public career but treating his private life with frustrating restraint. Frustrating because we do want to know. The most compelling parts of this book are the few times that the author gives us a glimpse of that world of which he was such an intimate part.

One such moment comes when he captures Sangster at the crowning moment of his career, when he returns to Vale Royal following his appointment as prime minister (which caught everyone by surprise; the account in this book serves as a good demonstration of the way Sangster outmaneuvered his rivals). This is how Neita evokes the aloneness of the most powerful man in Jamaica:

> Sangster walked from the car through the kitchen and dining room to the living room of the house. He greeted the household staff as he passed them. They did not know as yet, that he was now the prime minister. He sat with his press secretary and spent about 30 minutes discussing the schedule of appointments which had been set up...

and changes he intended to make in the Cabinet:

> ...With a parting, "See you tomorrow," Sangster walked slowly and carefully up the stairs of his residence to his bedroom, reading the Instrument of Office he had received from the governor-general 40 minutes or so ago. No wife, no mother,

no father, no sister, no brother to hug with joy and share this time of glory and congratulate him. The press secretary called the household staff together in the dining room and told them of Sangster's appointment. They applauded. He left them wondering who would move with the prime minister to Jamaica House, his new official residence....

Sangster did in fact have an extended family who supported him and several of his relatives have made a name for themselves in politics and other areas of public and cultural life. But apart from knowing that he had children, we know nothing of their mothers or his relationships with them and this book does not enlighten us. It certainly raises the question of how much we ought to know about the private lives of our leaders, dead or alive.

The value of this book lies in the way Neita has set out the life and times of one man in the context of a Jamaica transitioning from colony to nation and the major role he and others —now largely forgotten, too—played in it. Others such as Robert Lightbourne, Clem Tavares, Noel Nethersole, Wills Isaacs, or Rose Leon, to name a few who loomed large in the consciousness of Jamaicans of the Independence generation. A few of Sangster's political contemporaries have been immortalised in books. Neita has also written a biography of Hugh Shearer and much has been written by and about Edward Seaga, Norman and Michael Manley as well as Bustamante. But how can we praise other nation builders of the past and yes, those who presently occupy office, so they, too, might be known by future generations?

This is a book not only about Sangster but about who we were some 50 years ago. Neita's personal knowledge enables him to choose the events, personalities and anecdotes to highlight. Taking us back to those moments of, say, the actual Independence celebrations, is to remind us of what now seems almost a state of innocence.

And what of our hopes and dreams then? Sangster's first post-Independence budget was heavily in favour of agriculture and the focus was on the development of rural Jamaica. There was incentive legislation for industrial expansion; factories were being built. The stated emphasis was on local production and reduced dependence on imports. Which will lead every Jamaican to ask, what happened?

This is a political biography. But, it is also an instructive book about leadership, progress and a small island state taking control of its own destiny. The Sangster that emerges from these pages is a man who was a conciliator and a peacemaker, showing 'gumption and guts' but also manners and respect for others. A man whose public conduct might well be worthy of emulation by present and future politicians, and whose life, as presented here, might inspire us to regain our faith in the possibilities of politics.

—*Olive Senior, Author,*
The Encyclopedia of Jamaican Heritage

EDITOR'S NOTE

Hartley Neita's death, on December 12, 2008, left a void in the hearts of his family and friends. Indeed, it left a void in the minds of all who knew that they could call on him for his seemingly endless memory and unique ability to tell insightful stories, true stories, of the Jamaica he knew and loved so well.

So anticipated were these stories that the immediate and recurring lamentation after his death was, his other books in the pipeline would never be completed. Whether to counter or to quell these regrets, one friend remarked, "But Hartley was always midstream. No matter when his time came he would have left something unfinished."

Of all my father's projects, the biography of Sir Donald Sangster was the most complete. With a leap of faith and in an effort to fill the void, I took the decision to edit the manuscript and to get it published. An easy three-month project, I thought! After all, I had already helped him edit the first draft in 2006. My brother Gary delivered the files, and it was with mixed emotions that I read Hartley's assignment, "Michelle Neita—Editor". Digging deeper, it became clear that this was his second draft and that more time was needed. Thus began a labour of love that was to last some 18 months.

It was clear that Daddy had been working on improving the manuscript. It was now important to ensure that the research notes were accurately placed. In all, every effort was made to remain faithful to the facts, and to his style of communicating.

Special thanks to the Sangster family; to my siblings Gary, Karen and Gregory; my sons Graeme and Duncan; relatives and friends; to Lena Rose, of Minna Press, for her dedication; to Maxine McDonnough, for her calm clarity; to Michelle Welsh, who kept Hartley's imprint alive; and to Olive Senior, who helped maintain the integrity of the work.

PREFACE

Jamaica was a colonial territory of England from 1655 until 1962, when it gained its independence.

The head of the government was a governor who was the representative of the monarch of Britain. Its parliament was a Legislative Council which evolved in its composition over the years. By the 1930s this council was made up of a small group of officials who were heads of the major government departments and a number of persons, mainly wealthy businessmen, who were appointed to it by the governor. In addition, 14 persons, each representing a parish of Jamaica, were elected every five years to this council.

One such elected member was Peter Watt Sangster who served the parish of St Elizabeth from 1920 to 1935.[1] He was the uncle of Donald Burns Sangster who had a remarkable career in public life subsequently.

Donald Sangster became Jamaica's youngest ever elected representative when at age 21 he won a seat on the St Elizabeth Parochial Board, now known as a parish council. Later he became chairman of this board, the chairman in later years became known as the mayor.

He became Jamaica's first minister of finance after independence, acted as prime minister of Jamaica for nearly three years, and then became prime minister.

Yet, if you mention the name Donald Sangster to a group of Jamaicans under the age of 40 you are most likely to see a quizzical look on most faces. You will probably be then asked: "Donald who?"

But, ask about his contemporaries, Alexander Bustamante and Norman Manley, and the response by these same groups will be effusive. And this reaction is strange as for 18 years he was as dominant in Jamaica's national life as they were.

The reason for this was that he was a very private man. His biography in the various editions of *Who's Who in Jamaica* published during his lifetime was shorter than many others of lesser importance. There were just brief notes about his parents, his school life, his activities in sports, his brief career as a solicitor, terse mentions of his political life as a member and chairman of the St Elizabeth Parochial Board, a listing of some of his community activities and a few highlights of his career as a national politician and international statesman.

It was not that he was shy.

Modest? Yes.

Shy? No.

By nature, he was not flamboyant. He worked without any political fanfare. He believed in proving himself each day at whatever he did, and for that he was prepared to be judged.

He was a wealthy young man. He inherited hundreds of acres of land from his father on which he reared cattle, horses, mules, donkeys, goats, pigs and poultry. As an employer of labour he was, therefore, not involved in the early trade union movement. He treated his workers fairly and with respect so that when the island erupted in strikes in 1938 his properties were not affected.

Being far from Kingston where the political flames were first lit in the very late 1930s, Sangster was not broiled in this fire. His uncle, Peter, had been elected and re-elected to the Legislative Council between 1920 and 1935 before the advent of politics until he was defeated by a "grass-roots" politician, E.V. Allen.

Like his uncle, Donald Sangster believed that he did not need to be associated with politics. He thought that his personal popularity, derived especially from his activities in cricket and football as well as his involvement as an active member of community and parish associations would carry him into the new House of Representatives on a high tide of votes. After all, he was engaged in agriculture, tourism, the church, the scout movement, the public library service, plus his eligibility as one of the most sought-after bachelors in the parish.

So, he was indifferent to the founding of the first of these parties, the People's Political Party started by Marcus Garvey in 1930. And not being affected by the strikes of 1938, he did not see the effects they would have on legislative representation.

A strike early in 1939 by the workers at the Serge Island sugar cane estate in St Thomas, the eastern next-door parish to St Andrew, was the genesis of the other political movements, the

People's National Party (PNP) and the Jamaica Labour Party (JLP). The workers demanded an increase in their pay of ten pence per ton for cutting cane.

Bustamante, who was then a frequent public speaker in the city of Kingston agitating for better conditions for the working class and the poor, rushed to the estate to negotiate with the management on behalf of the workers. He had no mandate to do so, but his tall presence and dynamic personality gave him audience with the owners. He persuaded them to offer an increase of two pence to one shilling per ton to the workers.

This offer was rejected by the workers.

They continued the strike which threatened to become violent. The police was called to maintain peace but a clash occurred. Sixty workers were arrested. Some were given prison sentences and the others fined. They subsequently accepted the offer of one shilling per ton to cut the cane, and returned to work.

Bustamante could not take the credit.

Shortly after, there was a major confrontation between the management and the workers on the West Indies Sugar Company's estate in Westmoreland, the parish west of St Elizabeth. Once again Bustamante went there, this time as an observer. His return to Kingston coincided with restlessness among the workers on the city's wharves, the drivers and conductors of the buses and tram cars, the firemen and other groups.

Bustamante was everywhere. Night and day. He met with the employers seeking better wages and working conditions for their employees, and succeeded. Then, while walking to the Kingston Fire Brigade Station with his aide, St William Grant, they were both arrested and jailed.

Norman Manley, a cousin of Bustamante and a barrister-at-law of fame took over the negotiations and won an award of one shilling per hour for workers on the wharves. However, they refused the offer until Bustamante was released. He was freed. The men returned to work. It was the beginning of the Bustamante mystique.

Eight months later, on January 23, 1939, he founded the Bustamante Industrial Trade Union. Later that same year, on September 18, Manley founded the People's National Party.

At first, Bustamante was a member of the party, but he soon became disillusioned. He did not believe in being a follower. He had to lead, and being a member of the party he would be playing second fiddle to Manley. He therefore resigned his membership.

In the meanwhile, the strikes of the previous year led to the introduction by the British Government of a new constitution for Jamaica. Up to then, male voters had to be 21 years and over and they had to be paying taxes not less than ten shillings per year or be in receipt of an annual salary of at least 50 pounds.

Women were more restricted in their right to vote. They had to be at least 25 years of age. Like men, they had to be paying taxes of a minimum of ten shillings per year or be in receipt of an annual salary of fifty pounds. But most belittling for them was that they had to be literate and take a test in reading and writing, a requirement which was not imposed on men.

The new constitution which provided for universal adult suffrage gave every Jamaican, man and woman, over the age of 21, the right to vote. There were no restrictions regarding salary, the payment of taxes, gender or literacy.

In anticipation of the general elections which would flow from the improved constitution, Bustamante created the Jamaica Labour Party. It was launched on July 8, 1943.

The base of the party was the union and co-incidentally, most of the unionists were illiterate. This was unlike the People's National Party whose membership was largely drawn from the professionals and the middle class and was less than the overwhelming number of the new voters who would vote for Bustamante's party.

So said; so done. This new constitution came into effect on November 20, 1944. Nomination Day for the first general elections under this new constitution came nine days later. The elections were held on December 14.

The results were exactly what Bustamante expected. His party initially won 22 seats; the PNP won 4, and independents won 5 seats.[2]

Donald Sangster contested the South St Elizabeth seat as an independent candidate and lost. Manley was also defeated. For the next five years both continued their practice as lawyers, Manley as a barrister-at-law and Sangster as a solicitor. They appeared in a number of cases together and Sangster discussed the possibility of joining the People's National Party with Manley on a number of occasions. Sangster also continued serving as a member of the St Elizabeth Parochial Board.

He also reviewed his attitude towards politics. At first he considered joining the People's National Party but realised he would not be in the first tier of leadership which was occupied firmly by Noel Nethersole, Florizel Glasspole, Ken Hill and Wills O. Isaacs, all men of Kingston.

He was a countryman.

On the other hand, he did not see the same sort of competition from Bustamante's associates in the Jamaica Labour Party. He therefore joined the party and captured the South St Elizabeth seat in the 1949 General Elections which he had lost in 1944.

The assessment of his potential political fortune if he aligned himself to Bustamante proved correct. He was assigned the portfolio of Minister for Social Welfare and was appointed First Deputy Leader to the Majority Leader, Bustamante, in the House of Representatives. Fate next placed him in the dual posts of Minister of Finance and Leader of the House when Sir Harold Allan, who had been appointed to these offices by Bustamante since 1944, died suddenly in 1953.

It was these two offices which gave him the prominence he subsequently achieved, first in the international field of finance, and secondly as an influential leader in the parliaments of the Commonwealth of Nations and for which he earned the sobriquet, "Mr Commonwealth".

This is his story.

REASONING

O heart of mine, canst thou not be content
With all the glories life lays at thy feet,
The rosy dawns that unto thee are sent,
The laughing children with their faces sweet?
For thee the birds are singing in the trees,
Fair nature's beauties overspread the land
And thine are all the wonders of the seas.

Oh heart, what need is this that all earth's balm
Cannot assuage? What is this mighty boon
That thou wouldst have to bring thee perfect calm?
Thou growest weary of the years too soon:
Take thou life's gifts upon thy bended knee,
Naught for thy good will God withhold from thee.

—AUTHOR UNKNOWN

1 | OUT OF MANY

Jamaica's first five heads of government, Sir Alexander Bustamante, Norman Manley, Sir Donald Sangster, Hugh Shearer and Michael Manley, were cousins. Another of their relatives who served in Parliament was Douglas Manley.[1]

Many other relatives, fathers, sons and grandsons, husbands and wives and in-laws have also been members of Parliament.

There have, however, been more Sangsters than any other family who have served in the Legislature. The first was Peter Watt Sangster, who was the member for St Elizabeth in the Legislative Council from 1920 to 1935. Donald Sangster was the next, representing Southern St Elizabeth from 1949 to 1955 and North East Clarendon in the House of Representatives from 1955 until 1967. Later, their relatives, Astil, Kingsley and Derrick, also became Members of Parliament.[2]

Like many Jamaican families, the Sangsters were immigrants. The first two members of the family to come to Jamaica were brothers, John David Seivright and Charley, who were engineers. They were originally from Aberdeen in Scotland, but had been living and working in New York where they were recruited to work on sugar estates in the parish of Westmoreland in Jamaica. They became part of the melting pot of races which now make up the social kaleidoscope of Jamaica.

The original inhabitants of Jamaica were the Tainos. For hundreds of years these people were referred to as the Arawaks; and, because when Columbus arrived in the Caribbean in the 1490s he thought he had reached India, he and succeeding generations referred to them as Arawak Indians. Remnants of these people are said to still exist in the parishes of St Elizabeth, Westmoreland,

Trelawny and Manchester. Former Prime Minister and National Hero, Sir Alexander Bustamante claimed he had Arawak (Taino) blood in his veins.

During the following five centuries, many nationalities and races made Jamaica their home. These were the Spanish, English, Africans, Germans, Irish, Scots, French, Chinese, Indians, Syrians, Cubans, Haitians, Portuguese and Lebanese. More recently, small groups of Japanese, Filipinos, Russians and other nationalities, especially women, have migrated to the island and are gradually becoming more and more visible in the society.

The Scottish presence in Jamaica occurred in different migratory waves. Like the Irish, they arrived in the West Indies mainly as prisoners of war from the uprisings against Oliver Cromwell's rule. Many were forcibly taken to American colonies for sale as bondservants. After the capture of Jamaica by the British, Scots, described as idle beggars, gypsies and criminals were sent to Jamaica. There was also a great deal of voluntary emigration, some for religious reasons, and others for fortune or sheer adventure.

Not all Scottish migrants were from the lower class. Indeed, most of those who arrived after the 1740s were well-educated, middle-class men who came to seek their fortunes and return home to Scotland in the shortest possible time. Many were doctors, lawyers, estate managers and other professionals. Because of their colour, many were able to move up in the society and there were some who began as employees on estates and subsequently became the owners. The original Sangsters were examples of the latter.

After Emancipation, Scottish migrants formed part of the unsuccessful labour scheme to use Europeans to fill the labour shortage on the plantations created by the freedom of slaves. The scheme also included a plan to create European townships in the mountainous areas of Jamaica to spread White influence. The Germans were settled at Seaford Town in Westmoreland. No European township was ever created in the county of Middlesex.

Altamont in the Rio Grande valley of Portland was established, but many of the Scots who were settled there became ill and died, and their families went to live among the Maroons in Moore Town and Millbank.

Scottish surnames such as Kellier, Mitchell, Christian, Allan, Hepburn, Stephenson and Brodie are evident in these two Maroon villages and elsewhere in Jamaica. There are also place names in Jamaica, which are evidence of the Scottish presence such as Dressikie in St Mary, Blackstonedge and Edinburgh in St Ann, Aberdeen and Kilmarnoch in St Elizabeth and Glasgow in Westmoreland.

Because of this diversity of races in the population, "Out of Many, One People" was chosen as the National Motto of Jamaica when the country became an independent nation in 1962.[3] The choice was because of the many races and nationalities which make up the population, and the mix of cultures and religions that were infused in the society. Interestingly, Donald Sangster was the chairman of the Consultative Committee which was the body responsible for making the preparations for Independence. It was this committee which had the task of promoting the new National Motto as one of the important symbols of independent Jamaica.

2 | OWNING MANY PROPERTIES

The production of sugar from cane was the major industry in Jamaica when the Sangster brothers, John and Charley, came to work in Jamaica.

Rural society then was divided between an employer class which was mainly White, and the employed, the majority of whom were Black. There were, of course, White men who were employed as bookkeepers and overseers on properties. The Sangster brothers, who were also employees, realised that one qualification to be on the topmost rung of the ladders of social status was to become the owners of land and employers of labour.

Charley decided to remain in Westmoreland where he bought property on which he developed a sugar cane estate. John went to live in St Elizabeth where he bought Fullerswood, a property of 812 acres beside the village of Mountainside about five miles from the capital, Black River.[1] Cattle, horses and donkeys were reared on this property. There were also cashew and pimento trees.

Properties in St Elizabeth were then sold by auction.[2] The bidding took place on weekends when property owners got together for purchasing various estates such as Vineyard, Hermitage and Brownfield. On these weekends they gambled, drank and ran the auctions. Fullerswood was one such property which came up for auction. It had been idle for a number of years following the murder of one John Sawyers, by his slaves.

John Sangster was said to be a crafty bidder, keeping quiet during the drinking and gambling and bidding, then making his bid when everyone else had made their offer. Legend says he paid for Fullerswood and other subsequent properties with gold which he had brought with him from the United States of America, and which he kept in a thread-bag.[3]

A mainstay on the Fullerswood property was logwood, a native of Central America which was brought by seeds from British Honduras—now Belize—on the recommendation of Island Botanist Dr Barham. British Honduras was then a dependency of Jamaica, and the logwood, which grew there wild, was shipped through Jamaica to Europe, where dyes (red-purple, orchid-blue and black) were extracted from the heart of the trunk for use in the textile industry.

When slavery was abolished in Jamaica in 1834, large areas of fertile lands reverted to secondary woodland which contained logwood. By 1897 when banana planters re-cleared their lands, logwood was Jamaica's most valuable export, exceeding sugar and coffee. "Peak production for logwood was 115,000 tons in 1889," according to Patrick Bryan in his book, *The Jamaican People—1880 to 1902*. Scores of men were employed at Fullerswood cutting the trees, stripping the bark, loading them on to mule carts and taking them to the harbour at Black River where wharf owners such as Hendricks and Company shipped the logs to Europe.

Black River enjoyed significant wealth from the export of logwood. Its harbour was always full of cargo ships until the industry was torpedoed when chemical dyes replaced dyewoods.

Donald Sangster and his elder brother Louis Sangster inherited Fullerswood when their father William Sangster, a descendant of John, died. Louis was bequeathed the portion of the property known "by the name of Bennett Piece and Ruinate containing 208 acres with all the buildings thereon". In addition, he inherited portions of Alscott Pen known by the name of The Commons, Samms Piece, Hungerford, Road Piece, Top Road Piece, Nation Piece, Barbary Hall Piece, Guinea Corn Piece, David Piece, Paddock Hill Piece and Hermitage". Louis and Donald were also bequeathed "the mountain property in the parish of Westmoreland known by the name of Carrawina Mountain", and the livestock and rolling stock on the properties were willed for the use and benefit of their mother and themselves.[4]

He also inherited the lands known as The Orchard, along with a property called Brown Berry and parts of Alscott called Posapan, Old Ground, Top Posapan, Kitchen Piece and Kellis Piece. He also inherited the portions of Fullerswood known as Salt Spring, Bamboo Pot Piece, Goras Piece, Mullings Piece, and Cornwall.

Donald Sangster was born at the Victoria Jubilee Hospital in Kingston on October 26, 1911. His father was a commissioned land surveyor. His mother, Cassandra, nee Plummer, was a sister of Sophie, a former wife of Alexander Bustamante. The Plummers lived at "Marie Villa" on Church Street in Kingston.[5] It is therefore interesting to note, as observed earlier, that the first five heads of government of Jamaica since universal adult suffrage in 1944— Norman Manley, Alexander Bustamante, Donald Sangster, Hugh Shearer and Michael Manley—were related—a sort of royal family.

He grew his young years in a great house on the Fullerswood property near Mountainside. The house was at the end of a driveway of about a mile from the main road. A neighbour, George Davis, recalled that the property had scores of mango trees—"common, black, stringy, number eleven, turpentine, thin-skin, and other varieties".[6] He remembers that whenever he went by the house, Mrs Sangster always invited him inside for cake. She churned her own butter from milk from the cattle farm. Meals were cooked on a large Caledonia firewood stove over which there was a chimney. The house is now in ruins but he recalls it was very large, with walls made of cut-stone, fancy pillars on the verandah "and you walked up a flight of many stairs into a large living room".

The family, even after his father died on May 5, 1927, had several housemaids, the chief being Miss Lilly. No one in Mountainside ever knew her surname. They had a driver—a Mr Eustace Daley nicknamed "Moneyman". In those early years, cricket, cycling and other sports were held at Samms Common, a property owned by the Sangsters.

George Davis also recalls that Mountainside, the name of the neighbouring district, was the centre for holiday picnics and sport, drawing crowds from Top Hill, Black River and Malvern. Later, this sports centre moved to "Ballground", on lands donated by Donald Sangster. The new cricket field was opened with a cricket match between Mountainside and a team from Black River of which E.V. Allen, a future political opponent of Donald Sangster, was a member. Lands were also given by him to construct the present primary school and the Anglican Church Hall.

Mountainside, as the name suggests, spreads itself in the afternoon shade of the Santa Cruz Mountains. Former resident Derek Dyer, who became a permanent secretary and later managing director of the Jamaica Public Service Company, boasts of its peace and beauty. The village square at the junction of one road from Black River to Malvern, and another from Santa Cruz to Southfield and Treasure Beach, had the usual features of small villages elsewhere in Jamaica. There was a blacksmith, tailor, drug store and barber, a postal agency where everyone met in the late afternoons to collect his or her mail, and a Chinese grocery shop and bar which was the common meeting ground for the men of the village on Friday and Saturday nights.

Another common meeting ground was the St Augustine Anglican Church on Sundays. The Sangsters had a family pew in the church. Donald's mother was territorial of this status and was vigilant in preventing it from being used by others. Memory in the village today is of a member of the local gentry who once attempted to capture a seat in the pew. Cassandra Sangster who was present at church every Sunday stood, her arms akimbo, her eyes glaring. Wisely, the gentleman chose another pew.

Those who knew expected her to be present at church every Sunday, to protect her territory.

Rain or shine, in sickness and in health, her son, Donald, sat beside her.

There was no public electricity in the parish. A family, the Leydons, had installed an electric lighting plant in their house in Black River.[7] The families of Mountainside saw these bright lights when they visited the town at nights and wondered for many, many years, when this marvel would reach their village. There were also no telephones.

Few Jamaican towns then had domestic water supply systems, much less villages. And, because Mountainside suffered from drought for most of each year, water for household use had to be sparingly used. Most of the water came from the brief spells of rain, and was collected from gutters around the roofs of houses and channeled into drums, barrels, and tanks. Despite this little water, this community of small farmers grew a wide range of vegetables such as tomatoes, carrots, thyme, pepper, cassava, melons and corn.

Olive Senior's description in her book *Encyclopedia of Jamaican Heritage,* of the techniques the farmers used to water their crops, is most instructive.

> It is called fly penning, and mulching, using the savanna grass which grow profusely in the area after rain. The farmer cuts the grass and spreads it thickly in an enclosed field where he puts his livestock to provide manure. He plants his crops in the enclosure and removes the animals when the plants appear. The process is repeated in another small plot.

"By this means," she adds, "several crops can be grown during the year with even a little rain".[8]

3 | THE YOUNG YEARS

Donald Sangster was baptised at the St George's Church in Kingston.[1] His uncle, Peter Watt Sangster, who subsequently became a member of the Legislative Council for St Elizabeth, was one of his godparents. The other was Ernest Cooke, a family friend. His uncle was to have a major influence on the young boy, especially after the death of his father when he was only 16 years of age.

He began the discipline of education when he attended Sunday School at the St Augustine Anglican Church in Mountainside. At age seven he entered the elementary school in the district, the headmaster of which was Charles Blake. When he was ten years old he began his secondary education at Munro College in nearby Malvern.

Munro was then one of three grant-aided secondary schools for boys in rural Jamaica. The others were Cornwall College in Montego Bay, St James, and Beckford and Smith's in Spanish Town, St Catherine. There were also co-educational schools in rural Jamaica—Titchfield High School in Port Antonio and Happy Grove High School in Hector's River, both in Portland, Manning's High School in Savanna-la-Mar, Westmoreland, and Rusea's High School in Lucea, Hanover.

Munro[2] was founded from funds bequeathed by Robert Hugo Munro in his will of 1797. The funds were placed in trust to his nephew, Caleb Dickenson and the church wardens of the parish of St Elizabeth, to provide for the endowment of a school to be erected in the parish for the education of as many poor children in St Elizabeth as the funds could maintain. Hampton School for Girls, was founded later in Malvern.

To be admitted to Munro, boys had to be between the ages of 10 and 12. For admission they were examined in reading, education, the first four rules of arithmetic (simple and compound), the outlines of the geography of Jamaica and Europe, the classifying of words under their parts of speech, and the leading facts of the Old and New Testaments. Boys were also examined in French and Latin accidence, vulgar fractions, practice and interest in arithmetic; but failure in French and Latin did not disqualify them for selection.

The college had excellent buildings, which included a chapel, large dormitories, a library and classrooms, good playing fields, and a gymnasium. The main games played were hockey and athletics during the first term, January to April, cricket in the second, April to July, and football in the third, September to December. Secondary games were gymnastics, rifle shooting, tennis, badminton and boxing. John Gyles who became minister of agriculture and lands during the 1960s was the champion heavyweight boxer of the school during his last two years there.

Donald Sangster was a natural athlete. In his earlier years he ran and roamed through the acres of family property, chasing horses and other animals. Residents at the time who are still alive describe him as a people-person. "He moved around the property, mixed easily with all the workers, milked cows, rode horses, and ate on cook-outs with the workers," one resident recalled recently.

By the time he went to Munro he had developed an athletic frame with strong legs and lots of lung-power in his chest. He was also a healthy young man, drinking as he did a quart of cow's milk every day and eating lots of fruit, and fresh beef, chicken and eggs from the property.

In the first school athletic sports in which he participated at Munro as a Class 3 Under-14 Boy in 1924, he won the 100 yards in a time of 12⅘ seconds, the pole vault at a height of seven feet and the hurdles in a time of 20 seconds. He placed second in the 220 yards and third in the long jump and he was the Class 3 champion.[3]

In 1927, he was in Class 2 and won the four-mile cross-country race in the school sports, and also came first in the 220 yards, pole vault and the hurdles.[4]

At the 19th renewal of the Inter-Secondary Schools Track and Field Championships at Sabina Park in Kingston in 1928, he tied with Herbert McDonald of Calabar High School, A. Bennett of St George's College and W.F. Sinclair of Wolmer's Boys' School for second place in the High Jump Class 1.[5]

In the following year, 1929, he won the 220 yards and 440 yards, placed second in the 100 yards and pole vault and third in the mile at the annual track and field school sports at Munro.[6] And, at the 20th renewal of the Inter-Secondary Schools Track and Field Championships at Sabina Park held shortly after, he placed second in the 120-yards hurdles Open.[7]

Donald Sangster was in Calder House during his stay at Munro. In cricket, he was captain of the house team and the opening batsman. The school records show that in 1928 he averaged 35 and topped the batting average in the house cricket competition. In one match against Farquharson House he scored 60 in the first innings and 70 in the second. And against Coke House he scored 45, but Calder lost the match.[8]

On June 16 in that year Sangster won the toss in a match against Dickenson House and elected to bat. The school magazine reported, that "patient and careful cricket by Sangster supported by his team, wore down the Dickenson House attack. He made 38 in about one hour". The match continued the following day and Sangster continued batting to score 48 – the only batsman to make over 20 runs. Unfortunately, Dickenson knocked off the score.[9]

In representing Munro at cricket, Sangster opened for the school in a match against Santa Cruz and was caught by no less a person than B.B. Coke for 21 off the bowling of S.B. Birthwright.[10] Coke, as did E.V. Allen, figured later in his life as a political opponent. In describing his ability as a cricketer, the editor of the school magazine described him as "a defensive bat who is hard to dispose of in spite of playing forward with a very crooked bat, the danger of such a strike being minimised by reaching out to smother the ball. He has a very safe pair of hands in the outfield, but a trifle slow". He also represented Munro at boxing and gymnastics.

Later in 1949, he represented the old boys captained by Roy Lawrence, RJR's sports editor, in a two-day match against the present boys. He opened the batting and scored 35. His batting partner was his first cousin, Alfred Sangster who scored seven.[11]

He also became captain of the St Elizabeth Nethersole Cup cricket team. In one match against Trelawny on June 23, 1949, The *Daily Gleaner's* sports reporter in the following day's edition of the newspaper, praised his "dogged batting" of 21 not out with Garth Schloss' 101 not out in a last wicket stand which carried the St Elizabeth score from 83 to 210 runs for 9 wickets in their team's first innings reply to Trelawny's 90 all out at Siloah.[12]

Ken Parchment, who played for the St Elizabeth team as a pace bowler when he was a teenager under the captaincy of Donald Sangster, recalls that Sangster took the parish team to Kingston every Easter to play against Senior Cup teams such as Kingston, Melbourne and Kensington.[13]

Despite his wide-ranging sporting activities at school, his academics were not placed on the backburner. This was evident when he placed second in the island in 1927, in the Senior Cambridge (University) examinations[14]—the equivalent of today's CXC exams. He had already sat for and passed the Junior Local Examination of the University of Cambridge in 1925 in the subjects of religious knowledge, English language and literature, history, Latin, French, geography, algebra and chemistry.[15] At the end of his school career, he passed the Higher Schools Certificate Examination. His school reports while at Munro reveal a student who did very well in a wide range of subjects, and one who was determined to excel. He kept these reports and certificates all his life. It was his belief that people should keep records of their activities, not necessarily for their own gratification but for future generations to know who and what they were, and of any contributions they made to human endeavour.

He boarded at Munro. The family chauffeur came to the school for him on Saturday evenings after he completed whatever sporting activities he was involved in, drove him home for the weekend and returned to the school with him on Sunday afternoon. Many weekends his closest friends went along with him to his home.

He also spent time during many of these weekends at his Uncle Peter's home, especially after his father died.[16] During the summer holiday of 1929 after his father's death, and the summer holiday of the following year, Donald travelled through the parish with his uncle as he carried out his legislative council duties. He became intrigued from this young age of 17 at what was a turbulent interaction between the people and his political relative. His uncle tried to dissuade him from going into politics, but he was on public platforms throughout the parish campaigning for him in the 1930 general elections and confessing to Evon Blake, the publisher and editor of *Spotlight* magazine that "the greatest thing in the world is to speak on a political platform". His uncle won. He was "the happiest boy in the world".[17]

On graduating from Munro, he could have become part of the landed gentry – managing the family property with its cattle and other animals, bee keeping, and becoming engaged in the export of logwood. Of course, not everything involved in operating a cattle farm was pleasant. Alfred Sangster recalls that in those days one of the problems associated with rearing cattle was black leg infection:

> We used to control the black leg on the feet of the cows
> with a dressing of bluestone and lime and jeyes on the sore
> that the cows would get from flies laying eggs in them and

maggots emerging. To dress the cows you had to tie them up, and if necessary tie their feet. It was a risky business at times. Sometimes when you let loose the cows after they were treated they would chase people and try to butt them because of the pain they were feeling. It was quite a scary business. Then there were the ticks and grass lice in the pastures which left your feet full of pimples from their bites; and the only way to get rid of them was to break off a branch from a pimento tree and beat off the ticks and lice.

These were the messy aspects of farming that Donald Sangster did not like. Yet, farming was what his uncle, who had become a father-figure to him, wanted him to do. He, on the other hand, felt the tug of politics and it was the direction he wanted to pursue. Peter Watt was beginning to become disillusioned with politics, and on more than one occasion pleaded with his son Alfred, as well as his nephew, "to keep clear of politics". In addition, legislators were not paid then; one of the few concessions they enjoyed was the pleasure of riding first class on the railway from Balaclava to Kingston and return, which Watt did when he had to attend sittings of the Legislative Council.

And, as it is today, he had to provide loans to constituents, which were rarely repaid, assist others in financial difficulty, and help to solve the exaggerated expectations of people. Being a legislator was a financial drain.

Alfred Sangster heard his uncle say that up until then—in three previous elections—his political opponent was one F.C. Tomlinson, a barrister-at-law, whose conduct, he said, "was gentlemanly and whose courtly attitude in making platform references to him, his rival, had evoked the admiration of all". That had changed and racist slurs and a campaign of "colour-for-colour" were injected into the political dialogue.[18]

These warnings did not deter the young man. Politics was his choice; earnings from his property could more than sustain him while he indulged in politics and other community and social welfare programmes to better the lives of the people. In addition, he decided to seek a profession, one which would provide him with the skills to assist the poor and the needy.

He chose law, and became articled after leaving high school to Mervin T. King, a lawyer practising in Black River.[19]

The home where Donald Sangster grew his young years in Mountainside, St Elizabeth, is a site of historic national interest.

4 | THE CALL OF POLITICS

For four years, Donald Sangster learned how to take statements from clients and prepare conveyances, mortgage documents, contracts, leases and all the tedious details required of a solicitor. He found it fascinating, especially when he sat in court and listened to cases being tried on which he had done the preliminary work. He also studied bookkeeping and accounting through correspondence courses while pursuing his legal studies and obtained the Senior Commercial Education Certificate in these subjects from the London Chamber of Commerce, and certificates from the Institute of Bookkeeping, Classes 1 (Fellows) and 2 (Associates).[1]

He continued his interest in politics while studying and became Jamaica's youngest-ever elected representative on June 21, 1933 when at age 21 he won a seat on the St Elizabeth Parochial Board (now renamed parish council). He was also one of the spokesmen in his uncle's unsuccessful campaign for re-election to the Legislative Council in 1935 when E.V. Allen defeated him.[2]

In 1937, he came first in Jamaica in the final solicitor's examination.[3] He was 26 years old. He continued playing cricket for Mountainside, and he joined the Black River Football Club and played for that team. Horses he bred on his property such as Lalun, Dora Dora and Dora Dean were exciting turfites at meetings promoted by Willis and Spencer Hendricks at Gilnock and the Lower Works racetracks in Black River. The latter is now the site of the Black River High School.[4] Mrs. Joyce Francis of Black River recalls that he was "an avid race fan and was always at the race tracks".

Socially, he is remembered as a fabulous "cheek-to-cheek" dancer. Dances and parties were held regularly at the court house in

Black River and at the property houses in the community of towns and villages in the area.[5] Prominent families then were the Mullings, Rogers, Vassells, Blakes, McKnights, Patricks, Daleys, Binns, Leis, Brooks, Richards, Wrights, Grindleys, Essens, Clackens, Robinsons, Dyers and the Laurie Smiths.[6] Older residents remember the dances held by Elijah Barrett at his residence in the middle of the Black River square.

Music at these dances was often provided by the Baba Motta and Val Bennett orchestras from Kingston. Donald Sangster was a young and eligible bachelor and was very popular with the girls. Mothers regarded him as the ideal son-in-law. He was wealthy, he did not smoke and was only a social drinker. He was a casual but neat dresser. He was also courteous, polite, and gracious. He was a charmer.[7]

Donald opened his law practice in Black River, upstairs the present Courts Furniture building on High Street. Shortly after he was approached by Joyce Lawson, now the Hon. Joyce Robinson, and told of the need for accommodation for the St Elizabeth Parish Library. He gave the space on the ground floor of his office for this facility, rent free.[8]

He also had an office in Santa Cruz. He became known as "Lawyer Sangster" and residents in his home village, who used other lawyers or could not afford one, often discussed their cases with him, for free.[9] One of the cases he undertook was to represent Oscar Palmer of Queensbury, Southfield in St Elizabeth, who was charged with praedial larceny of 100 roots of cassava, the property of Leopold Hanson. Lawyer Sangster successfully questioned the evidence of identification presented by the Crown and Palmer was accordingly dismissed.[10]

He recruited Lilla Patrick of Rich Pen, a district near Mountainside, as one of his secretaries after she graduated from the Black River High School. A highlight of her work with Sangster was when she sat in court in Balaclava during a case in which he had briefed the legendary Norman Manley. She was fascinated with the way Manley questioned opposing witnesses and confused them.

She remained with Sangster until he died. She recalls he was "like a father and a brother combined to me. He was kind, considerate, very nice and a good lawyer." Another of his secretaries was Lily Morgan.

In 1938, workers all over Jamaica, in cane fields, sugar factories, and at the ports, went on strike. There were also many riots. St Elizabeth was spared the brunt of this revolt. There were, however, some minor strikes in Black River, Malvern, Balaclava and Santa Cruz, but these were quickly settled, unlike in neighbouring Westmoreland where a turbulent upheaval on the West Indies Sugar Company's factory and farm lands took place.

There was no trouble on the Sangsters' properties, probably because Donald Sangster was seen as a "good mixer and approachable at all times by all persons of whatever level". He was also kind and very thoughtful about the welfare of the workers on his property.

One resident recalls. "Every Christmas him kill a cow for us workers and for the old people in the village, and him sit with us and him eat with us. Him treat we fair with good wages, too."

General elections should have been held in 1940 but because of the World War, it was decided to postpone these elections. With no such elections in the offing, Donald Sangster fixed his attention on parish issues and needs. He had already been an assistant commissioner of scouts, the president of the St Elizabeth branches of the Jamaica Agricultural Society, a trustee of the Munro and Dickenson Trust, a lay member of the Anglican Synod, a member of the Black River Drainage and Irrigation Board, member of the Manning Home Advisory Committee and of the East and West St Elizabeth School Boards.[11]

Sangster was a foundation director of Jamaica Vegetables Ltd. between 1943 and 1949. This was an organization founded by Colonel R.W. Moxsey. Other directors were R.W. O'Neil Speid and

Bertram Henry, and they pioneered the growing of export vegetables from Jamaica, helping to transform southern St Elizabeth from being one of the country's poorest districts, producing mostly cassava and congo peas, into the bread basket of Jamaica. They developed the technique of mulching, and exported millions of kilos of tomatoes, and produced carrots, pumpkins and other vegetables for the local market.[12]

Sangster was also a member of the Board of Governors of the Institute of Jamaica. And, he was not just a member by name but he was active in the programmes conceived by these organizations.

He got his foot on the second rung of the political ladder in 1941 when he was elected vice-chairman of the St Elizabeth Parochial Board.

In the meantime, according to a political reporter in the *Daily Gleaner*:

> The people of Jamaica were being gradually mobilised at two social levels: at the trade union level under the leadership of Alexander Bustamante to make new economic advances for wage-workers; and at the political level under the leadership of Norman Manley to make an independent nation out of a 300-year-old colony. Donald leaned sympathetically to both movements but remained on the sidelines.[13]

Two years earlier, for example, he was ambivalent about which of the two political parties he should join. He held discussions with Norman Manley about joining the People's National Party,[14] and he agreed to a request by Manley to preside at a meeting of some 200 persons in the village of Brompton, St Elizabeth. The meeting was addressed by journalist Vere Johns and actor E.M. Cupidon who invited them to "throw their whole weight behind the party". After the addresses and discussion that followed, Sangster called for a show of hands to the appeal. The response was spontaneously unanimous in favour of the formation of the Brompton Group of the People's National Party.

He did not pursue any further interest in the People's National Party and for some time he shunned the Jamaica Labour Party.

Politics, however, was to pursue him.

Following pressure, principally from the Clarendon Legislative Council member, J.A.G. Smith and the People's National Party, the British Government approved a new Constitution for Jamaica in 1944. It offered Jamaica the first step towards independence. This new constitution was proclaimed in all the parish capitals and it gave the island representative, though not responsible government. It provided for a wholly elected House of Representatives of 32 seats based on universal adult suffrage, presided over by its own speaker; and a Legislative Council which was partly ex-officio and partly nominated by the governor. Also coming into existence was an executive council of ten members, five chosen by the leader of the majority party in the House of Representatives and five by the governor from the Legislative Council. This council, which was presided over by the governor, was to be the principal instrument of government policy.

General elections took place in December 1944. The Jamaica Labour Party, the People's National Party, the Jamaica Democratic Party, other minor parties and a number of independents contested it. Donald Sangster chose to contest the South St Elizabeth seat as an independent candidate.

He launched his campaign with a crowd of about one 1000 persons, with representatives from every district in the constituency. These were described as "Committee Representatives from a wide cross section of different social and economic groups". Included on the platform was F.C. Tomlinson who had been his uncle's opponent in all the elections he had contested. E.V. Allen, who was also contesting the elections in the neighbouring constituency of Northern St Elizabeth, had been invited but he sent a telegram "expressing regret for his absence and wishing every success for the Conference".[15] Allen was the current member of the Legislative

Council for St Elizabeth having defeated Peter Watt Sangster in the 1935 elections.

B.B. Coke of the Jamaica Labour Party with 3,783 votes won the election. Second was Malcolm Hendricks, who was an independent candidate and who obtained 3,601 votes. Donald Sangster came third with 3,500 votes. Incidentally, E.V. Allen, who also ran as an independent in the neighbouring constituency, was defeated by N. Cleve Lewis of the Jamaica Labour Party.

Undaunted, Sangster turned his attention back to the concerns of the people of Mountainside and the parish. He became, for example, the secretary of a Tourism Development Association for the parish. He was convinced that tourism could play a major role in the economic development of the parish.

The committee was established to develop plans for tourism attractions such as fishing in and boating on the Black River, and creating a look-out point at the spectacular Lovers' Leap 1,600-foot tall cliff.

The association also examined proposals for mapping the caves in the parish with the intention to encourage visitors interested in speleology to explore them. There was, for example, a cave at Mexico near Balaclava which is probably the longest in Jamaica; it is nearly one mile from the One Eye Gulf to Mexico Gulf (the mouth of the cave). The One Eye, which is the name of the early miles of the Black River, passes through this cave which had been explored for some distance but because of some deep holes of water obstructing the passage, less was known of it than other caves. There was also the Peru Cave near Goshen with its very beautiful stalactites and stalagmites, the Yardley Chase Caves at the foot of Lovers' Leap, the Wallingford Caves near Balaclava, and the Pedro and Hounslow Caves where there were Taino (Arawak) remains.

He wanted to establish a craft centre at Bamboo Avenue where souvenirs made from bamboo could be sold, climbing Spur Tree Hill at the border of St Elizabeth and Manchester, horse-back riding, swimming at the foot of the Y.S. and Maggotty Falls, and the improvement of the mineral bath at Lower Works near the town of Black River as additional tourist attractions.

This spa at Lower Works was very popular in earlier years but because of the long distance from Kingston and Montego Bay, and the poor state of the roads, it had begun to lose much of its popularity.

There was also a cemetery in the village of Hodges with dozens of tombstones of Shakespeares, and the committee initiated a search for a link between these families and William Shakespeare of Stratford-upon-Avon in England. Nothing concrete came from the enquiries, but members felt that the Shakespeare name could be an attraction to curious English visitors.

In addition, there were white sand beaches between Black River and the border of the parish with Manchester. Discussions had therefore taken place with owners of these beachfront lands at Billy's Bay, Frenchman's Bay, Calabash Bay, and Great Pedro Bay, to encourage them to build villas and cottages on these properties to attract tourists who preferred idyllic holidays in private villas, as he once said, "far from the madding crowds in large hotels". He believed that St Elizabeth was better suited for cottage complexes built in proximity to attractions.

He also believed that the development of a tourist industry in St Elizabeth would benefit the many craft producers in the parish. In his travels in subsequent years he saw the association between craft and tourism, with craft items being produced as souvenirs. He always brought back souvenirs from his travels for his friends and members of his staff.

The craft industry was very vibrant in the parish, and he saw its potential. Both men and women were involved in craft production; the men were involved in doing the heavier work of cutting, curing and transplanting raw material. The women were mainly involved in weaving. Children often helped them when they were not at school.[16]

The district of Southfield was the centre for a straw industry where baskets, hats, handbags and other useful articles were made. In a recent television interview on the CPTC television programme, *Hill and Gully* which was produced and presented by Gold Musgrave Medalist Carey Robinson, Corlette Johnson, a craft producer living in Top Hill, described the wide range of straw products which were made from plants such as long thatch which grows in the hilly areas of the parish, big thatch in the Santa Cruz Mountains, Hodges, Lacovia, Brompton and Newmarket, silver thatch which was found in the Santa Cruz Mountains and the Pedro Plains Hill, sisal and river-rush which were found in Middle Quarters and lace bark which was obtained from a tree which grows in the Cockpit Country. The Cockpit Country is an area, largely uninhabited in north St Elizabeth and south St James, consisting of conical-shaped hillocks of steep valleys with a rich diversity of flora and fauna, many of which are endemic to Jamaica.

Corlette Johnson and members of her family produced beach bags, fans, shopping bags, hats and other items from straw and which were once marketed through Things Jamaican, a government agency. The straw used by her and other producers in St Elizabeth provided an income which enabled parents to educate their children. In earlier years, too, girls at secondary schools such as Hampton in St Elizabeth, St Hilda's in St Ann and St Hugh's in Kingston wore straw hats as part of their uniform and these were mainly made by the craft producers in the parish. Other products made by these craft producers were hampers for donkeys, floor mats and rope.

Dyes made from the sap of trees and shrubs were used to colour the straw. Many of these trees and shrubs grew on Donald Sangster's properties, and he allowed his workers to make dyes from them in their free time. Blue dye was made from indigo; red dye from annatto, hibiscus, tamarind and beet; yellow dye from beet, chrysanthemum, cotton, onion, pomegranates, spruce, sunflower, tomato and fustic; marigold dye from turmeric; green from onion, parsley, fustic, iris and giant cane; brown dye from coffee, cotton, fustic, tea, tobacco and Indian hemp; and black dye from Indian hemp. There were also factories at Lacovia and Elim where the dye from logwood was extracted.

When Edward Seaga created the Jamaica Festival Commission to encourage the development of craft, and Things Jamaican Limited to market this craft, Donald Sangster was able to put these agencies in touch with the craft producers in St Elizabeth.

Reminiscing about these projects in later years with Director of Tourism John Pringle and his press secretary, Hartley Neita, Donald Sangster as acting prime minister noted that the parish had more natural attractions to appeal to visitors than did the then resort areas of Montego Bay, Ocho Rios and Port Antonio. He told Pringle about the groundwork which had been done by the St Elizabeth Tourism Association to identify the possibilities of creating a tourism presence in the parish. Pringle subsequently visited the parish on a number of occasions and recognised Sangster's assessment of the possibilities for tourism to be well founded. However, Pringle explained to him that his priority was to fill the hotels in Montego Bay, Ocho Rios and Port Antonio before attention could be paid to St Elizabeth.

Pringle did, however, persuade the transport operators in Montego Bay, and Ocho Rios to a lesser extent, to provide opportunities for tours to the parish to some of the attractions Sangster's Tourism Development Association had identified.

5 | FROM PARISH TO NATIONAL POLITICS

Sangster was elected chairman of the St Elizabeth Parochial Board in 1949. He also became chairman of the Jamaica Social Welfare Commission, the government agency which had replaced Jamaica Welfare Limited.

The second general election under universal adult suffrage was imminent. Alexander Bustamante had won the first elections by a landslide, but support for his party was waning. He recognised that some of the men who had been carried into the House of Representatives on his coattail had not proved to be capable representatives. During the first five years, he had to rely almost entirely on Frank Pixley, a lawyer, and on Portland businessman Harold Allan who, though not a member of his party, had served him well as leader of the House and minister for finance.

Bustamante set out to find more men of Pixley's and Allan's background and calibre. His choices were his protégé Hugh Shearer, a trade unionist, Rose Leon, a businesswoman, Allan Douglas, a solicitor, businessmen and farmers Felix Toyloy and Andrew Ross, Tacius Golding and Joseph Z. Malcolm, teachers, Rev. S.U. Hastings a minister in the Moravian Church, and Donald Sangster who had run as an independent candidate in 1944 and finished a mere 283 behind the winner in a field of five.

In the 1949 general elections Hugh Shearer and Rev. Hastings lost. Sadly for Bustamante, too, Solicitor Frank Pixley, the man who had been his right hand during his first term, lost his Central Kingston seat to Wills O. Isaacs of the People's National Party.

The Jamaica Labour Party won these elections, but with a smaller majority. Donald Sangster ran against Claude Blythe of the People's National Party, and independent candidates B.B. Coke, Edmund Broomfield and Percival Hutchinson.

This time he won.

Donald Sangster was assigned the important social welfare portfolio replacing Bustamante's previous right-hand man Frank Pixley. Other appointments were Isaac Barrant as minister of agriculture, Joseph Z. Malcolm as minister of education, Sir Harold Allan as minister for finance and general purposes—and leader of the House. Bustamante took the portfolio of Communications. Speaker of the House was O. Alphonso Malcolm. One year later, Sangster was elected first deputy leader of the party and served in that office for 17 years.

Sir Harold Allan died on February 18, 1953. He was preparing the Budget when he died. Allan had been a former member of the Legislative Council for Portland prior to 1944 and was therefore the most experienced of the parliamentarians up to the time of his death. He had subsequently successfully campaigned twice as an independent—in 1944 and 1949. Each time he was elected he had wisely thrown the weight of his 23 political years and his influence with official government, with the Jamaica Labour Party, and had been rewarded by Bustamante with the prestigious portfolio of finance. On Allan's death, Sangster inherited the finance portfolio as well as the added responsibility of leader of the house.

In his subsequent role as the opposition spokesman on finance after the JLP's defeat in 1955, Sangster was not like his colleagues on the opposition bench who resorted to shouting their arguments in debates in the House in the belief that if you talked louder than your opponent you were the victor. Instead, he was analytical in his critique of speeches by his opposite ministers of finance, Noel Nethersole who died in 1959—also while preparing the Budget—and his successor Vernon Arnett.

The late Hector Wynter, who was parliamentary secretary in the Ministry of External Affairs while Sangster was acting in later years as prime minister and minister of external affairs, had a high regard for Sangster's debating skills. He noted that Sangster's arguments were conversational "without resorting to hysterics". Former Prime Minister P.J. Patterson did not serve in Parliament while Sangster was alive but had attended meetings of the House from time to time as an observer and heard his presentations. Patterson recalled:

> He was an excellent debater, marshalling his facts in an orderly manner and presenting them with logic. His training and experience as a Solicitor provided him with a background that stood him in good stead in Parliament.

One of Sangster's favourite haunts was the Press Club on Water Lane in Kingston. Many of his free nights saw him there discussing national issues with the journalists of his time. There was Theodore Sealy, the powerful editor of the *Daily Gleaner*, other members of the staff of this newspaper—Eddie Williams, Jack Anderson, Calvin Bowen, Vic Reid, Percy Trotman, Ivorall Davis, Hector Bernard and lone female Aimee Webster, Hal Glave of the Government Public Relations Office, Evon Blake of *Spotlight* magazine, Esther Chapman of the *West Indian Review*, Peter Abrahams of the *West Indian Economist*, H.P. Jacobs of *Public Opinion*, Len Nembhard of *Jamaica Times*, Alva Ramsay of *The West Indian Sportsman*, Elsie Benjamin of *Pepperpot* magazine, and free lancers such as Vere Johns and E.H.J. King. The discussions were not confined to politics, but included music, art, sports, industry and all aspects of Jamaican life.

Donald Sangster also loved the magic of the theatre. His son, Bindley, recalls his father taking him and other members of the family to a pantomime at the Ward Theatre.[1] Donald tried to see as many plays as possible at the Ward, the Garden Theatre on Hope Road, the Little Theatre on Tom Redcam Avenue and the Creative Arts Centre at the University of the West Indies, Mona. His wide circle of friends included actors and actresses such as Louise Bennett, Ranny Williams, Lois Kelly, and Carmen Manley, directors and playwrights like Slade Hopkinson, Sylvia Wynter and Derek Walcott, and producers Paul Methuen and others. He also tried to see at least one play in London and New York while he was in those cities.

Perhaps it was this affinity with the theatre that led him to resort to the dramatic in some of his budget speeches.

In one, after analyzing and dismissing the budget which was presented by Nethersole as "junk", he calmly raised his copy of the budget and proceeded to tear out the pages, one by one, and commenting as he threw away each page that "the figures presented are not worthy of the pages on which they have been printed."[2]

On another occasion he charged that the government's revenue budget had brought widespread tax and price increases on the poor, and that the government was unable to do anything to ease the problems of poverty, unemployment and rising cost of living. Then he displayed two coil springs on the table before him. The larger spring he said represented the spiraling cost of living, and the shorter showed "the puny rise in working class income".[3] Incidentally, his son Bindley was in the Strangers Gallery that day, along with his class mates from the 6th Form of Jamaica College.

In another year, he compared the economy of Jamaica to an inflated balloon. To describe the inflationary policy being pursued by the government and the danger to the economic health of the country, he took a red balloon from his pocket, blew it up then pricked it with a pin. There was a loud pop as it burst. A photographer from the *Daily Gleaner*, Astley Chin, who was in the House and had received the permission of B.B. Coke, the Speaker, to take photographs, took a flashlight picture of the scene.

Ken Sterling, the parliamentary secretary in the Ministry of Trade and Industry was quickly on his feet protesting that Sangster's blowing up of a balloon in the House was shameful and lowered the dignity of the House.

The Speaker rapped his gavel demanding silence. When he gave Astley Chin permission to take photographs of the proceedings of the House, he had not expected him to be in cahoots with Sangster.

"I debar further picture-taking," he said. "We are not here for that. I don't want that picture to come out in the *Gleaner*."

Chin started to leave the public gallery. The Speaker called to him. "I repeat. Let that cameraman listen to me. Please stop there. That picture must not be published. In fact, I want that film confiscated. I am quite serious about that."

By then, Chin was on the verandah and was racing down the steps and into Duke Street. The Speaker stood and kept rapping his gavel. "Let that cameraman listen to me," he shouted. "Please stop right there. I repeat the picture must not be published. In fact, I want the film confiscated."

He called an orderly. "Stop that man," he said. "I want him to bring back the film."

Along with a policeman, the orderly chased Chin down Duke Street. Meanwhile, the Speaker kept fuming. "If that picture is published in the *Gleaner* I will assert my authority as Speaker of the House."

A few minutes later, the Speaker was advised that Chin had been caught. He adjourned the sitting and had the photographer taken to his office where he confiscated the camera.

At the end of the afternoon's sitting, the Speaker commented on the issue. He said that when he gave permission for a photographer to be present he did so because he did not feel that he should be wedded to the pattern of other parliaments in the Commonwealth where such privileges were more often withheld than granted.

> I have never denied a request to permit photographers in the House because I believe they are making a contribution to honest, democratic principles. However, privileges in this House are not for the purpose of permitting what I regard as cheap buffoonery which does not add to the dignity of the House.

Then, in an obvious reference to Sangster, he added:

> I deeply sympathise with those persons who would bring into ridicule their own beloved parliament, not caring how much of our prestige and dignity may be sacrificed as long as they can achieve some childish or impish aim. I shall not permit

the clean atmosphere of this House to become fouled by the introduction of any foul odour. This Honourable House is a place of honour and that it shall remain.[4]

Sangster ignored the comment.

The following day the camera was returned to Chin.

The production staff of the *Gleaner* was then on strike, and the *Gleaner* did not resume publication until two weeks later. To Coke's surprise and anger the photograph that Chin had taken and a story of the incident was published on its front page.[5] Chin had removed the film on which the photograph was taken and replaced it with another before handing it to Coke.

The Speaker was not pleased. To add to his discomfiture, he received a letter from the Jamaica Press Association upbraiding him, shortly after. The letter said it regarded as "high-handed and a severe threat to freedom of the Press, his action in seizing a camera belonging to the Gleaner Company Limited which was used by cameraman Astley Chin to take a photograph of the Opposition Spokesman on Finance inflating a red balloon while speaking in the Budget Debate". The association said that his action in granting permission for photographs to be taken in the House and then seeking to withdraw that permission after the photograph was taken "amounts in the view of the association to be an attempt of censorship which is not to be tolerated in a free democracy such as ours".

Once again, the Speaker was not pleased. That night at the Press Club, Theodore Sealy teased Sangster, describing his antics as that of "a frustrated actor".

6 | MR COMMONWEALTH

Donald Sangster's rise in the party was quick. He was soon elected first deputy leader of the party "by virtue of his ability, his devotion, and his dedication to the cause of Jamaica". Within the party he was rated *primus inter pares*, and according to *Spotlight* magazine, he towered majestically over his comrades. The magazine added: "In JLP's ranks, Lawyer Sangster is way above his colleagues in ability and in performance. Whereas he operates on the statesman's level, they being run-of-the-mill people have been mediocre politicians".[1]

Sangster was appointed as Jamaica's chief delegate to the Commonwealth Parliamentary Association. As such, he went to the association's conference in New Zealand in 1950. The public saw these conferences as opportunities for parliamentarians "to see the world at the expense of taxpayers". Not so, Donald Sangster. Before going to the conference he sought a brief from the officials in his ministry and the Ministry of Finance and General Purposes on relationships between Jamaica and other Commonwealth countries.

For him, it was not just another trip. Through his direct contact with Prime Minister S.V. Holland of New Zealand, a ban on Jamaican cigars which had been in place since 1938 was lifted. In addition, the volume of fruit juice importations was increased and the rum quota increased.[2] Not only that, some years later, he secured from Harold Holt, the Australian prime minister, an undertaking that Australia would import more spices, annatto and rum from Jamaica. He also initiated discussions with Prime Minister John Diefenbaker of Canada, regarding a proposal for a development loan to finance the construction of schools in Jamaica. In talks with Canada's Ministry of Trade he also cleared the way for a larger two-way flow of business, and secured a liaison office for West Indian students in Ottawa and Washington D.C.

He also made his mark at the conference for plain speaking.

"The West Indies," he told delegates at the plenary session, "do not presume to dictate policy to the Dominions of the Commonwealth. All we ask is an opportunity to present a picture—as we see it—of the problems in the area".

And he did. He showed how the West Indies' economy was originally based on sugar and rum, of how it had developed to include oil, gold and bauxite, of how the standard of living was incompatible with that required in civilised countries, because, over the years, "the West Indies has not enjoyed a just return for our labour commensurate with the price we have to pay for the labour of the manufactured goods we have to purchase". He cited the policy of the United States of America with countries with which that country was politically associated; and he saw no reason why in the Commonwealth the policy should not be the same.

Continuing, he recalled the exploitation of the West Indies by the early British settlers whose sugar fetched them as much as £100 per ton, and their failure to plough back some of this wealth into the islands.

And with industrial development as a cure for West Indian economic life, he made a loud call for more capital investment, and told how the governments of the region were willing to grant facilities and incentives which would make investment safe and sound.

The delegates gave him a loud and sustained ovation. The concerns about which he spoke were echoed by others at the conference and by leaders of developing countries more and more in the future. It was the beginning of an impact on Commonwealth-related issues which continued for another seventeen years, and which subsequently earned him the title of "Mr Commonwealth".[3]

7 | WINNING AND LOSING

For a number of years, the British Government kept prodding its colonies in the West Indian islands, British Guiana and British Honduras to become a federal union. The political heads had discussed the idea informally at various times, but it was not until October 1947 that Britain succeeded, for the first time, in bringing the leaders of all the British Caribbean peoples together in Montego Bay, St James, to give the matter official consideration. The conference was presided over by Arthur Creech Jones, the British secretary of state for the colonies. Representatives of the governments of Jamaica, Trinidad & Tobago, Barbados, the Windward Islands, the Leeward Islands, British Guiana and British Honduras attended. From their pronouncements it appeared that the region's leaders were basically pro-Federation, though some had slight personal and other reservations.

One such was Bustamante.

The governments of Trinidad & Tobago, St Vincent and Grenada subsequently voted acceptance of the principle, but for four years the issue of whether or not there would be a federation teetered and wobbled. The governments of the other smaller islands watched as Jamaica fiddled fitfully. Federation went on the legislature's agenda twice but was never debated. The Jamaican Government led by Bustamante seemed to be listless about Federation; Norman Manley and the People's National Party displayed a more enthusiastic interest.

To put the islands on an integrated economic base as a prelude to Federation, the British got the West Indies to set up a Regional Economic Council. Donald Sangster who was the most articulate supporter of the federal idea in the Jamaica Labour Party was put on this council as Jamaica's delegate. Still, the impetus towards Federation was sluggish. The greater political concentration, especially by the JLP, was reserved for local affairs. In fact, the JLP Government seemed fairly satisfied with Jamaica's semi-colonial structure, while the opposition PNP kept up pressure for further constitutional changes that would hasten the move towards independence.

Then came Sir Hugh Foot as the new governor in 1951. In his inaugural address to the legislature on April 7, he underscored the importance of Federation for priority action. To him, it was "Federation or frustration".

He then began to press both parties to move towards the Federal goal with the first constitutional amendment that brought real responsibility to the people's representatives being the inauguration of the ministerial system under which eight of the electives took charge of all the government departments except for the police, the army, the judiciary and external relations. The first five selected by Bustamante were Isaac Barrant, Agriculture; Lester Simmonds, Education; Rose Leon, Health and Housing; Lawton Bloomfield, Communications and Works; Donald Sangster, Finance; and of course Bustamante, Chief Minister.

Progress came. A debate on a motion in the House to "accept the principle of Federation" was led by Sangster. On August 4, 1951 in a rare coalition vote, the House of Representatives went overboard in its support for Federation. After the vote, Bustamante said: "I and my cousin (Manley) will work out the details. We must move on, and move quickly." Manley's comment was more elaborate: "When all the difficulties, obstacles and fears are removed," he said, "the central fact remains that the totality of the Caribbean area has the capacity of becoming a sizeable unit in the world and developing a voice that will be heard in the councils of the world, provided it is an independent voice and can speak in its own right."

The debate on the motion "to accept the principles of Federation" was led by Sangster. "Jamaica," he said passionately," "is going to make up its mind once and for all not only to sponsor Federation, but to take its proper place in the leadership of the Caribbean area."[1]

Jamaica's sudden ardour—or more appropriate, Bustamante's—was not due to Foot's nudges alone. In part, it had been generated by anger over an Anglo-Cuban Pact, under which Britain gave Cuba generous trading concessions for their sugar and tobacco which were detrimental to Jamaica. As Jamaica saw it, the deal was a stab in the back.

Sangster was livid when he told Britain's overseas trade secretary, Arthur George Bottomley at a meeting of the Regional Economic Conference in Barbados in May 1951, that "Britain must scrap the pact, have nothing more whatever to do with it no matter how vile you may look in international eyes. Our children are entitled to have protection and we must get it. For too long we have been pawns in the international game of chess. We wish promotion to knights and bishops."[2]

It was felt that Britain should have at least acquainted the country and the other Caribbean islands beforehand. Indeed, had there been a Federation of the British countries in the Caribbean, they could have switched a considerable portion of its trade elsewhere in reprisal, a possibility Britain could not have ignored.

The "Black Pact", as this British deal became known, was a disguised blessing for the Federation.[3]

8 | BALANCING THE BOOKS

Apart from the Federation issue, it was at this time that
Donald Sangster began to come into his own as Leader of the House
and Minister of Finance. Before, he had been operating in the shadow
of the late Harold Allan who had been handling the portfolio for
nine years. Interestingly, too, it was he who presided at the first
Cabinet meeting of the five members. Bustamante was attending
the Coronation of Her Majesty Queen Elizabeth II in London. The
meeting was held at Headquarters House on Duke Street in Kingston
on May 26, 1953.[1]

By November 1954, he was selected by *Spotlight* magazine as
the "Man of the Year". The cover story, which highlighted what was
described as a stellar performance in his role as Leader of the House,
referred to him as:

> ...a statesman while his colleagues remained mere politicians.
> Where other Ministers blundered, floundered or faltered under
> the new and onerous responsibility of relating the present to
> the future, he drove a straight path; his assurance and zeal
> spread confidence all along the line, won the nation's applause
> and even the Opposition's support.

Listing his other achievements, the magazine noted he had
successfully persuaded members of the House to agree to night
sessions in order to get more work done, and guided the Constitution
Reform Committee to a far-reaching interim report. The report
reflected his own dogged struggle with King's House for the transfer
of full administrative powers to the people's elected ministers, and
his demand that the attorney general and colonial secretary should
be ousted from the executive council and their powers handed over
to elected ministers, an agreement which he won.[2]

To his ministry he had brought a pool of brilliant civil servants, most of them young, and drew deeply on their advice. Given the opportunity for the first time to use their talents and abilities without fear of being squashed from the top, these young minds helped to guide the new ministerial system and make it work. Men like G. Arthur Brown, J.E. Clare McFarlane, Gladstone Mills, Percy Beckwith, C.H. Dinroe, Hector White, George Phillips, Herbert Saddler, Kenneth Pinnock, Neville Glegg, Robert Mason, Ronnie Matthews, D. "Jack" Clarke, C.F. McDonald, Dennis Goldson, Louis McKenzie, C. St C. McDonald, R.A. "Jack" Harrison, and female officers such as Mary Winch, Marguerite Smith, Una Samuda, Madge Smith, Carmen Roberts, Lois Birthwright, Fredericka Edwards, Julia Mowatt and Cynthia Frankson, worked into the long hours of night, on weekends and public holidays.[3]

When Sangster succeeded Sir Harold Allan as minister of finance after his death on February 18, 1953 he did not have enough time to put his own stamp on the budget which was due for presentation two months later. However, in the following year, 1954/55, he gave the country a budget which was not just the dust-dry compilation of anticipated revenue and expenditure that was characteristic of previous budgets, but was seen by journalists covering the event as a masterful chart and compass aligned with a recent World Bank Mission report, to guide the country for the year ahead and beyond.

According to *Spotlight* magazine this budget "startled in projecting a staggering £19½ million expenditure in one year, the biggest ever". Budget increases had been the fashion for years. They had risen spectacularly from a modest £2½ million in 1938 to £7½ million in 1944, to £10 million in 1949 and £14⅓ million in 1951. In fact, the sharp, swift up spurt in spending and earning had even outpaced costs as the official Cost of Living Index showed—100 percent in August 1939, 324.8 percent in April 1954.

Designed as a please-all, the budget intrigued even the opposition.[4] It carried no increase in taxes, yet provided for salary boosts to civil servants, subordinate staffs, daily workers, and the police and school teachers. It created many new posts, and charted an accelerated pace for several works projects. As an instrument to win friends and influence votes in an election year, it had everything.

Even to businessmen it seemed a clever manipulation of "needs against availability"; it chartered big bold expenditure in a period of inflation and likely trade recession.

And more than anything else, it balanced, even though the £9,000 surplus was small.

Spotlight magazine observed that in his budget speech:

> Sangster warmed up to the task like a man conscious that the historians had their notepads out. He knew he was making history in many directions at once. One was the size of the expenditure. Second, the budget was the first to be fashioned by the Ministry of Finance while tailored by the Cabinet. Thirdly, it was the first with so much spending, so many concessions, and no tax increases. Fourth, it was the first time that an elected member had the duty of stating government policy and reporting the state of the nation to the nation.

In two-and-a-half hours, Sangster detailed the items in the Budget, meticulously showing alterations, amendments and improvements over previous budgets. With no taxes, how then would the budget be financed? By the fourth day of the debate, Sangster came to the House with a request for £100,000 advance on loans to be raised. It was the first pointed indication of how he would balance the budget, and of how his new economic policy would work, as opposed to old methods of financing. How? By paying for development projects and programmes out of loans which would be paid for by future generations—the people who would benefit most from them.

It seemed good policy. The opposition could find few holes in it.

All in all, the year 1954 was a good year for Sangster, and Jamaica. He had established the Ministry of Finance as the central ministry of government, insisting—for example—that all Cabinet submissions with even the most minimum financial implications had to be cleared by the Ministry. He had also piloted a £30 million, five-year development plan through the Legislature.

Industry, encouraged by the policies he outlined in his budget presentations and public demand for its products, went on a show with an 11-day, 100-display trade exhibition that drew 120,000 visitors. Banana exports, zeroed by Hurricane Charlie in 1951, went to 19 million stems, the highest since the dizzy 27 million peak in 1937.

Politically, the Jamaican Constitution made a giant stride when the ministries were increased from five to eight, with the ministers given full executive and administrative powers. George Headley was appointed elementary schools cricket coach, and Herb McKenley appointed supervisor of Jamaican athletes. The first Hi-Lo Supermarket was opened in Cross Roads, St Andrew. Jamaican 4-H Club representatives to England's Young Farmers Club Festival —Keith Roach and Milton McNichol—won the Queen's Silver Cup for best judging. A Miss West Indies, Jamaican Evelyn Andrade, entered the Miss Universe beauty contest at Long Beach, California for the first time and won plenty of praises, but regrettably no prizes. Education Minister Lester L. Simmonds and a *Gleaner* news reporter, Vincent Truman, were each sentenced to 15 months imprisonment for selling state secrets. And, Kingston port worker, James Williams, alias Harbour Shark, won £10,000 in the Jamaica Sweepstake while in debtor's cell for non-support of his wife.[5]

The following year, the People's National Party defeated the Jamaica Labour Party in the general elections of January 1955. The polls opened at 7.00 a.m. and by 5.00 p.m. when they closed, 495,680 of the electorate (65.1%) had voted. Counting continued until long past midnight. As it did in the previous elections, the *Gleaner* erected a giant score board at the Kingston Race Course. The many thousands in Kingston and St Andrew who did not own radios, crowded around it to follow the blow-by-blow account of the contest.

In South Clarendon, where Bustamante was contending with the PNP's Charles B. Murray, the Chief finished with the biggest individual score of all 106 candidates: 13,668 to Murray's 8,946, a positive sign that though his party was defeated, his own prestige was still aces high.

In East St Andrew, where Manley was up against the JLP's Wilton Hill, the PNP Leader won with 11,854 to Hill's 7,881.

In West St Andrew, where the JLP's Rose Leon, the Farmers' Party's Gwen Edwards and the PNP's William Seivright had each worked frenziedly for victory, it was Leon with 13,265 who won the seat. Seivright gained 11,639, while Edwards lost her deposit with a paltry 660.

In West Kingston, Hugh Shearer with 6,383 votes defeated Iris King of the PNP who received 5,246 votes, and Ken Hill of the National Labour Party, 3262.

Donald Sangster was one of the casualties. He faced the heavy odds of schoolteacher B.B. Coke's combined personal following and PNP backing, obtaining only 7,835 votes to Coke's 11,769. With his frequent absences abroad on national and regional business, he had not given enough attention to the needs of his constituents. They ignored his international, Commonwealth, and regional status. Coke who had been actively wooing voters ever since 1949 when Sangster nosed him out of parliament was swept back in with a comfortable margin of 3,934 over Sangster. Coke had originally won the seat for the JLP in 1944. He had however, quarrelled with Bustamante and resigned from the party in 1947, ran and lost as an independent in 1949, but now made it back with the PNP.

9 | BACK IN THE SADDLE

After he lost his seat in the House as the Representatives for South St Elizabeth in the January 1955 general elections, Donald Sangster accepted Bustamante's invitation to lend assistance to the Bustamante Industrial Trade Union (BITU).[1] Hugh Shearer, his "main man" in the union, was elected to the House of Representatives and Bustamante needed someone capable and whom he could trust to supervise the union's work while he and Shearer attended to opposition business in the governing of the country. Sangster lived and opened legal offices in an annex of the Melrose Hotel on Duke Street in Kingston, which was conveniently close to the offices of the BITU. His secretary was still the faithful and loyal Lilla Patrick.

The new PNP Government took office in mid-February 1955. With only six weeks to present a budget by April, there was not enough time to prepare a budget which reflected the "The Time for a Change" theme which was the slogan of its election campaign. Recognizing this, Sangster offered to brief Noel Nethersole, the new minister of finance on the line he had pursued and the concepts which formed the budget he had prepared.

PNP supporters were disappointed and angry when they discovered that the budget subsequently presented by Nethersole had preserved financial skeletons of Bustamante's private enterprise government. Not only that, but Nethersole publicly acknowledged Sangster's assistance and thanked him for having briefed him.[2] Yet, despite Nethersole explaining that of necessity the budget could not include any element of the party's ten-year-old "Plan for Progress" such as the cherished state bank which would promote its economic development programmes, the voice of reason and knowledge was not heard in the babel of their sound and fury. It took some time for them to resign to the fact that for a while in a democracy the new PNP Government would have to live with JLP skeletons in its closet, however loud they rattled. And it would be the same if the roles were reversed.

Just before the budget presentation, the JLP was shaken when the Attorney General's Department issued summonses alleging election breaches for Rose Leon and George Peryer. Leon had won a seat in West St Andrew and Peryer had won the North East Clarendon seat, both for the Jamaica Labour Party. The breaches were in connection with incidents alleged to have taken place at a meeting in support of Peryer's candidature in Clarendon during the campaign for the elections, which took place the previous month.

Both were charged under the Section 83 (c) of the Representation of the People Law, in that they had made false statements against Percival Broderick, one of Peryer's opponents, about his personal conduct. The statement made by Peryer at Colonel's Ridge in Clarendon on Tuesday December 28, 1954 was that Broderick had received bully beef, condensed milk, shoes and clothes from Alexander Bustamante to distribute to people after Hurricane Charlie in 1951. Peryer then asked the audience if they had obtained any of these items and when they responded "No", he told them that Broderick had taken the goods instead to Smithville and stocked a shop he owned there.

Both were found guilty. Automatic forfeiture of their seats in the House of Representatives and disqualification as voters for five years were the consequences of their action. For Rose Leon, the irony was she had lost her safe seat as a result of helping Peryer to win his. Subsequent appeals by both were dismissed by the Court of Appeal.

In the meanwhile, Sangster had set himself up in residence and opened a legal office in Chapelton in Clarendon in case Peryer lost his seat and it became vacant. It did, and in a subsequent by-election held on December 7, 1955, Sangster defeated Broderick (7,083 to

5,374), and independent, politically-unknown businesswoman Verna Lee Bennett, and regained his seat beside Bustamante in the House. And sitting in the speaker's chair was none other than the man who defeated him in the last general elections in St Elizabeth, B.B. Coke. Both men smiled at each other when Sangster entered the House.[3]

Following his re-election, Sangster was re-appointed by Bustamante as the opposition spokesman on finance. He also became the party's chief spokesman on the proposed Federation of the West Indies.

He became a quiet apostle for the Federation. In August 1957, he expressed pleasure that the Federation was not only of interest to people in the West Indies but also to scholars outside the Caribbean region, and criticised the Manley Government for not providing the Jamaican public with more information about the advantages of federation. Later in the year he urged participation in the new state and encouraged contribution of the best possible material. In the long run, he felt, the Federal Government would have much to do, and said that persons who adopted the ideals of the JLP were best suited for the job of managing the Federation.

Despite his deep involvement in politics he never forgot his religious upbringing. For example, his mother had given him a pocket-sized Bible before she died. A family friend, S. Ormsby, had given it to her on May 20, 1894, inscribing in it: "To Satta Plummer—"grow with grace". It was beside his bed until he died and so used was it that many of the pages were loose.

It gave him strength in his faith.[4]

So it was not strange that he once found himself acting in the role of a peacemaker between the Christian churches. A controversy was taking place between the heads of the Church of England and the Roman Catholic churches in Jamaica regarding such "temporal and doctrinal issues as the primary designation and rightful See to the Bishopry of Kingston and the righteous reputation of reading the Holy Bible". Just recently, too, there was bickering between these two pillars of Christianity in England.

He was an ardent churchman and had grown up in the Anglican denomination. He had, however, many close friends in the leadership of the Roman Catholic Church, and indeed, all the denominations, and he was concerned that this religious dispute could end the hope that the Roman Catholics would join the Jamaican Christian Council. From time to time, he discussed the problem with these leaders without seeing the dispute resolved. He, therefore, decided to speak about it publicly hoping that in doing so both sides would respond by getting together to resolve the issue.

The opportunity came when he addressed the Paradise Baptist Church at Croft's Hill in his North Clarendon constituency in August 1957. There he urged the Christian community to be tolerant of each other, for, according to him, the Church had to play an important role in the Jamaican society and uphold the highest standards by setting an example of unity and cooperation for the masses and the country as a whole.[5] Sadly, he died before the Roman Catholics became part of this community of churches in 1971.

He also took stock of the reasons he had lost his St Elizabeth seat. One was that he spent too much of his time in Kingston on his ministerial duties, as well as abroad, and not paying enough attention to his constituency. This time he invited Andy Abrahams, a businessman and a member of a prominent family of Chapelton in Clarendon and his friend Clarence Chang to be his political aides and as a liaison between himself and the constituents. He rented office space for his legal practice and political activities from a tailor, Mr Humphrey near to the Chapelton Post Office. Later he rented a house at Ashley, and then purchased it.

Sunday was the day he set aside for meeting his constituents. This was after he attended morning service at St Paul's Anglican Church in Chapelton.

He employed Miss Daisy Thompson, a former school teacher as his political secretary in the constituency. He also made regular visits to the villages and towns, keeping in constant touch with the parish councillors and other leaders in the constituency and paying random visits to homes of his constituents, whether they supported him or not.

A home he visited regularly was Percy Broderick's.[6] Since they contested the seat in the by-election the two men had developed a close friendship. In addition, Broderick was the president of the Jamaica Agricultural Society and Sangster, who had previously been president of the St Elizabeth branches of the Society, had retained his membership in the Society, and with his earlier farming experiences on his property in Mountainside they had a lot in common. Broderick was also a successful farmer in Morgan's Pass where he lived.

From his meetings with his constituents and close working contact with Andy Abrahams and Clarence Chang, he was kept abreast of their problems.

The constituency had many farmers, large and small, and because of frequent periods of drought there were times when the lack of water affected their crops. Those who lived close to the Rio Minho and its tributaries suffered less. For household water, children woke early in the mornings and went to the river to take home pails of water on their heads. They also used the opportunity to bathe in the river, which was illegal. The provision of domestic water supplies in the constituency became a priority. Sangster made representations[7] and, in due course, was able to obtain a domestic water supply for residents in Prospect and Morgan's Pass, an expansion of the water supplied to Chapelton and some minor water supply projects in other districts.

Another problem, which he was able to solve, was that the Jamaica Government Railway intended to discontinue the railway service from May Pen to Frankfield. The railway was used by people who commuted to work and by children who attended schools such as Clarendon College. He negotiated a continuance of the service much to the relief of the people.[8] Later, too, when the railway authorities decided to cease carrying canes for farmers in upper Clarendon to the Sevens Sugar Factory near May Pen, he was able to persuade them to continue the service.[9]

Another project he began working on was for a bridge at Arthur's Seat in his constituency. This was finally constructed in 1964.[10] This bridge shortened the distance between Chapelton and Crofts Hill by 10 miles. He also successfully obtained the government's help to provide a road in the McNie and Douglas Castle areas of north east Clarendon and in St Ann. In this he received the support of the deputy speaker and member of the House for North West Clarendon, O.A. Malcolm, who described the roads in upper Clarendon as the worst in Jamaica.[11]

Most of the roads in his constituency were unpaved. Rain fell frequently in some areas and scoured these roads. During his time as the member of Parliament he was successful in his representations to asphalt the road from Summerfield to Beckford Kraal, Kupit Bridge to Morgan's Pass, Friendship and Colonel's Ridge, and from Trafalgar Hill to Cross Roads. He also persuaded the parish council to construct a parochial road from Summerfield to Cross Roads. Another road, too, was from May Pen Wood to Sevens Estate.

He was also able to get a community centre on lands previously occupied by a stud farm. This was opened on August 1, 1964.

Through his representations, too, a new tax office was built in Chapelton. He had the out-patients section of the Chapelton Hospital improved and a building constructed for an x-ray unit. He also persuaded the Ministry of Education to construct the Simon's and Mitchell Hill primary schools.

A monument to his memory is the Sangster Heights Housing Scheme near Chapelton. This was completed after his death. He also obtained a postal agency at Mitchell's Hill and another at Elim to serve the districts of Blackwoods, Windsor, Patton and Burrell Field.[12]

In 1960, Sangster was awarded a Leader Grant by the US State Department to spend two months in that country observing the structure and operations of the government at all levels, with particular regard for the financial side, the administration of justice, and the inter-relationship of federal, state and local governments. His main interest was the operations of the government as it was administered from Washington D.C. In his capacity as the former leader and more recently as a member of Jamaica's parliamentary delegations to various Commonwealth conferences across the world he had used those opportunities to observe the administrative institutions and practices of these countries. The Leader Grant enabled him to observe another type of operations in a non-Commonwealth country.

He was absent from the annual conference of the Jamaica Labour Party in December and therefore missed the drama of events when Bustamante unilaterally declared the elections of officers void, took sole control of the administration of the party for a few days and which led to the resignation of Madame Rose Leon as chairman of the party.[13]

One month later she also resigned as a member of the party.[14]

Anglican Bishop of Jamaica (1955-1967), The Rt. Rev. Percival Gibson, CBE, (foreground, second right) assists with the ribbon cutting for the bridge at Arthur's Seat, one of the many rural projects completed under the careful watch of Donald Sangster (right foreground) as Member of Parliament for North East Clarendon.

©The Gleaner Company

10 | JAMAICA, YES; FEDERATION, NO

Meanwhile, the new PNP Government accelerated the pace of the development of the Federation. The federal union was finally formally inaugurated in 1958 with Jamaica adopting a bi-partisan approach. Unfortunately, the prime minister of the Federation, Sir Grantley Adams of Barbados, threatened, among other things, to introduce a federal income tax, retroactively.

This was a red rag to the bull that was Bustamante; he who had always felt that Jamaica would be bearing the brunt of the cost of the Federation. He sent a cable to Adams warning him that the imposition of the tax could only happen if Manley won the next general elections. Manley immediately issued a statement to counter Bustamante's threat, declaring that "Jamaica will have to consider withdrawing from the Federation if the Federation contemplates policies disruptive of Jamaica's economic development".

Manley continued:

> The Federal Government has no power to levy income tax for the first five years and there can be no question whatever of the Federal Government doing anything of this sort, let alone making such legislation retroactive.

In an attempt to ease the federal strains that that had developed, Manley sought urgent changes in the federal structure. To accomplish this, two committees—the political and economic—were set up in Port of Spain, the capital of the Federation, to negotiate the changes. Donald Sangster, who was personally pro-federal on the side while wedded to the JLP's growing anti-federal stance, was a member of both committees and attended all the meetings as the JLP representative.

Then a series of events came which seemed to leap-frog

over each other. Robert Lightbourne, who was the JLP-affiliated Democratic Labour Party member of the Federal Parliament for the parish of St Thomas, abruptly resigned his seat in order to contest the Western St Thomas seat against the PNP's Kenneth Clarke in the general elections which were expected at any time. He won. And, for the vacancy left in the Federal Parliament, Edwin Allen who had lost his Clarendon seat in the last general elections was chosen to contest the St Thomas by-election.

On the eve of nomination day, Bustamante took an about turn. He announced that the Jamaica Labour Party would not be contesting the election. Furthermore, the party would seek to have Jamaica secede from the Federation if and when the JLP became the Government of Jamaica in the future. "Our decision that Jamaica should secede from the Federation is irrevocable," he declared.

Commenting on this statement, *Spotlight* magazine said:

> That Bustamante was no "federationist" was plain even in the 1947 Montego Bay conference. He had waspishly asked then what good could come of federating pauper houses...

And, continuing in its remembering the magazine recalled that:

> ...as Government leader and as Opposition boss since then, Busta, even while sending aides to pre-federal conferences, has veered from seeming acceptance, to irrational condemnation, to conditional and reluctant espousal of Federation.

Now he was making it plain. "I want Federation to mash up," he shouted.[1]

This was the end of the bi-partisan policy on Federation. Norman Manley had no alternative but to announce that his government would conduct a referendum to allow the people to decide if Jamaica should remain in the Federation or not. This referendum was held on September 19, 1961 with the JLP advising secession and the PNP advocating for the maintenance of the federal partnership.

Donald Sangster's personal views were support for the Federation, but he remained loyal to his party's policy in favour of secession. He launched the party's referendum campaign with a broadcast on Radio Jamaica Redifusion (RJR) on September 11. Federation, he said, was a dream dangled by Britain in front of West Indian politicians as a means to achieve independence and nationhood for small countries like Jamaica. He said:

> In the light of current world and Commonwealth politics it has become apparent that a country small in size and population can achieve Independence. Jamaica was always able and is more than able now to achieve that Independence and equality by herself for we have all the requirements of sovereignty.

He pointed out that the party had agreed to participate in the Federation during a five-year trial period. That trial, he said, had shown it would not help Jamaica now or in the future, and so "we put forward the view, come out while the coming out is good".[2]

Sangster made it plain that "coming out will not prevent Jamaica joining in regional activities. For example, the University College of the West Indies was a regional activity before political federation and would continue to be so after we come out of the Federation". He was followed each week with broadcasts by Edward Seaga, Robert Lightbourne, Rose Leon and Clement Tavares. He continued to play a major role in the referendum campaign and on referendum day voters returned a majority of 38,942 for secession.

It was the end of the Federation.

Both parties then sat together to draw up a new constitution for an independent Jamaica. The committee, which formulated the constitution, consisted of 17 members. They were Norman Manley, Alexander Bustamante, Wills O. Isaacs, Florizel Glasspole, Vernon Arnett, Claude Stuart, Iris King, Donald Sangster, D. Clement Tavares, Edward Seaga, David Coore, J.P Gyles, Robert Lightbourne, Douglas Fletcher, Neville Ashenheim, Rudolph Burke and the

Attorney General. Donald Sangster, because of his legal training and as the most politically experienced member of the Bustamante team was Bustamante's chief advisor at these discussions.

The report of the Joint Legislative Committee and the draft of the Independence Constitution were presented to the House of Representatives on January 23, 1962 by Premier Norman Manley. After a three-day debate the members of the House stood and gave unanimous approval to Manley's resolution asking approval of the report and the constitution. And, in a rare and unusual emotional moment of support and hope for the future, members of the public who had packed the public gallery and followed the debate during the three days also stood and shouted "Aye" along with the elected representatives.

It was against the rules of the House for the public to demonstrate in this manner, but the Speaker merely smiled at this breach of protocol.

11 | WINNING INDEPENDENCE

It was a grand moment, and for a few days everything seemed smooth sailing. But the wily old Bustamante was not one to allow this sweetness and light to give his supporters the belief he was losing his political touch.

The Secretary of State was asked by Manley to receive a delegation to discuss and approve Jamaica's request for Independence. He agreed.

But just before the joint delegation of four members of his opposition party and four of the government's was to leave, Bustamante announced he would not be traveling to London with the delegation. The other seven members were lesser lights. It was he, Bustamante, who had made this opportunity possible. It was he who insisted that Jamaica should abandon its flirtation with a federation with the other Caribbean countries. And it was he and his party who had defeated Manley and the PNP in the federal referendum.

He would therefore travel by himself. He would arrive in England as solus majesty.

He did not leave Jamaica until February 1, the day on which the British-Jamaican Conference began. Prior to embarking on his flight, Bustamante said to reporters:

> I see where Manley has suggested the first of August as our Independence Day. Queen Victoria of blessed memory abolished slavery in Jamaica on the first of August, 124 years ago. What significance has that with our Independence now?

His suggestion? From October 14 in the previous year he had declared that:

...there is only one historical date for Jamaica's Independence and that is May 23, 1962. For it was on that date in 1938 that the tide to move for freedom for democracy, for release from British rule, when tens of thousands of the working people marched throughout the island protesting against the dismal and indescribable conditions under which they worked and lived. It was on the 23rd of May 1938 when from on top of Queen Victoria's statue on South Parade in Kingston that I addressed one hundred thousand persons of all categories and classes. And it was on the 24th day of May, 1938, that I was thrown in the Police lock-up at Sutton Street jail where I was kept for three days and subsequently removed to the Rae Town prison.[1]

Independence would therefore be fixed in people's minds in association with the sacrifice he had made for them. He had been to jail for his people. He was a martyr.

Meanwhile, with the absence of Bustamante, it was Sangster who for the first two days led the Jamaica Labour Party's side of the Jamaican delegation at the beginning of the talks which were hosted by Britain's secretary of state for the colonies, Reginald Maudling. Following Manley's opening address to the conference in which he reviewed the process of bi-partisan participation which led to the presence of the Jamaican delegation at the conference, Sangster spoke in support and emphasised the determination of his party to return to Jamaica with an approved Independence Constitution.

He began by recalling that it was exactly 300 years ago that the first constitution was established in Jamaica. The then administrator, General Doyley, had been ruling under military law. In 1661, the committee of the Privy Council in charge of the plantations, made the constitution which was put into operation in 1662 by the same Doyley, who then became the first civil governor of Jamaica:

So, now in 1962, 300 years after, we are participating in the end of colonial rule on the island.

Britain has established in Jamaica democratic government under the parliamentary system and the rule of law—all great traditions which have taken a thousand years and more to be developed in England. That is one part of our heritage.

On the other hand, we are still an underdeveloped country. We are fighting hard to provide an improved standard of living for our people. We still have poverty, hunger and too high a level of unemployment. That is why so many of our people are coming to seek a living in Britain, and hence we are deeply concerned over the implications to us of your joining the European Common Market. That is the other side of the coin.

So as we meet here for these talks on the final steps to independence, our thoughts are many and varied. We have a heritage of democracy and a legacy of substandard living. Premier Manley has told you something about the events leading us to this Conference. I could add to what he said that Jamaica has been independent-minded for a long time. You only have to read the reports of parliamentary debates of 200 years ago to realise that even then the colonials of those days wanted their own way of life.

We started on this last road to Independence in 1938, but we paused on the way to help federation. Then in 1959 my party began the campaign to take Jamaica out of the federation. And here, let me borrow from the words of Brutus: 'It is not that we loved others less, but we loved Jamaica more'.

I am happy to say that the draft Constitution that we are here to discuss was prepared on a bipartisan basis in a remarkably short period of time, and in the present context of Jamaica's affairs broadly covers our needs. For along with this Constitution, we have political stability. We have created a two-party system of democratic government patterned on Britain's. We have accepted the rule of law. We are building up an economy as fast as we can with the means at our disposal. There may be differences of opinion as to methods, but there is no difference as to the objectives. Capital and labour are working together and although the trade union movement started only in 1938 it is now firmly established.

Finally, our civil service is of the highest integrity – a fact of which we are justly proud.

These things qualify us for Independence, Mr Secretary. We are not severing our connections with your Government and country. Indeed, we are seeking admission to the Commonwealth club as a Dominion. We live in troubled times. We see our neighbours in the Western Hemisphere confronted with difficult problems. Jamaica has chosen her clear choice for that way of life that provides freedom for the individual.

We are a small country, but we are geographically situated like a beacon on a hill whose light can be seen from far away. It is our hope that our faith and our conduct will inspire others to regain their faith in God, in truth, and in the sanctity of the rights of man.[2]

His comments were well-received and appreciated by Maudling and his advisers, and by Manley's half of the delegation.

By the time Bustamante joined the delegation in London, Manley and Sangster and their teams were in accord with most of the issues which had arisen. The gravity of the exercise mellowed Bustamante's fighting mood. Gone were the political growls he had left in Jamaica. In no time, he and Manley came together in a formidable combination which left Secretary of State Reginald Maudling, no space for maneuvering. When he proposed an October independence date, instead of the August date that Manley had finally persuaded Bustamante to accept, they brushed his suggestion aside and firmly insisted on August 6. That date was to be for the year 1962. Thereafter, it would be celebrated on the first Monday of August.

In his closing remarks at the end of the Conference, Bustamante injected a note of humour:[3]

I am happy that Mr Manley and I were able to work together as if there was only one party in Jamaica—the Jamaica

Labour Party. In a more serious vein, however, we go forward now to independence and a new association with Britain. Independence, however, can only be meaningful if we can achieve for all our people a standard of living which will permit them to live in dignity and self-respect. With this objective in view, we move forward with the firm resolution of making Jamaica the greatest little nation on earth.

The camaraderie ended immediately after they signed the agreement with the British Government. Each booked flights for their return to Jamaica on separate planes. Before leaving his hotel, Manley held a press conference at which he announced to British newspaper reporters that general elections would be held in Jamaica on April 10. It was as he had done where the referendum was concerned. The people of Jamaica should decide which party they wished to lead them into independence.

No Jamaican reporters were present.

Manley and his team of Vernon Arnett, Dr Ivan Lloyd and Florizel Glasspole arrived at the Montego Bay International Airport at noon. There was no welcome fanfare. Manley confirmed to the *Gleaner's* north coast reporter, Alvin Wint, that the elections would be held on April 10 as he had announced in London. Wint wondered, to himself, why he had not made the announcement in Jamaica. He decided not to ask him directly.

Manley and his colleagues drove directly to Kingston via Ocho Rios. Two hours later, Bustamante, Sangster, Robert Lightbourne and Clement Tavares arrived at the Montego Bay Airport and were welcomed by a crowd of bell-ringing supporters. They remained in Montego Bay overnight and returned to Kingston the following day via Lucea, Savanna-la-mar, and May Pen, holding celebration meetings along the way.

It was the beginning of another election campaign.

12 | A NATIONAL FLAG

Jamaicans had been tossed and turned in a political maelstrom during the preceding years. Before 1958, Jamaica was a colony. Its flag was the red, white and blue Union Jack of Britain; its anthem was "God Save the Queen". Then for two years it had a Federal Flag, and was on the verge of becoming a West Indian nation. In fact, it had teamed with other British West Indian countries at the 1960 Olympic Games in Rome. And still sang the British national anthem. Suddenly, the Federal Flag had been thrown aside. Once more it was a colony; its anthem was "God Save the Queen" again.

Manley felt that the first government of the Jamaican nation should enjoy the full loyalty and trust of the people.

Logic said that his party would win these elections. In the federal elections held in March 1958, the Bustamante-led West Indies Democratic Labour Party won 12 seats in Jamaica to five won by the West Indies Federal Labour Party, led by Manley. In July 1959, 15 months later, however, Manley had called general elections for the Jamaican House of Representatives and decisively defeated the Bustamante party with a count of 29 seats for the PNP and 16 for the JLP. True, two years later the PNP with its support for federation, had been embarrassingly swamped when 256,261 people voted against remaining in the federal body while 217,319 voted for Jamaica to remain in the federation.

Manley believed, however, that while Jamaicans had become wary of federating with countries and people with whom they were never really close, they had become confident that the PNP had their interests and a better programme for the development of the country than the JLP.

On the face of it, there was logic. But politics and logic are like oil and water. They are not compatible. So, in the elections, the Jamaica Labour Party won 26 seats while the People's National Party went into opposition with 19 seats. Once again, Sangster returned to his old portfolio of Finance.

Independence was only four months away. A lot of detailed preparations had to be made. Some had already been taken care of. Manley, in his wisdom, had appointed a committee in the months before he lost office to prepare for the occasion and the attendant celebrations. For its chairman he chose editor-in-chief of the *Gleaner* publications, Theodore Sealy. Vice-Chairman was Allan Morais of the Office of the Premier, a civil servant of the highest integrity. Other members were selected from a range of interests, education, business, social work, the news media, the university, the legal profession and the arts. Three other government officials were also included, H.L. Lindo, the governor's secretary, P. W. Beckwith, the number two official in the Ministry of Finance and A.G. Langdon, acting deputy commissioner of police.

A secretariat of a small group of other government officials led by B. St J. Hamilton in the role of administrative secretary was also created. They were to submit recommendations to a consultative committee set up under the chairmanship of Premier Norman Manley, to plan an appropriate programme of events to celebrate the achievement of independence and to coordinate the island-wide activities to mark the occasion. The Consultative Committee consisted of Manley, Donald Sangster, Dr Glendon Logan, the Minister of Welfare and Culture, and Sealy.

By the time the government changed hands many decisions had been taken. Among these was the adoption of National Symbols for Jamaica. For the National Bird, the swallow-tail or streamer-tail hummingbird, which is endemic to Jamaica and incidentally is the second smallest bird in the world; the National Flower, the *lignum vitae*; the National Fruit, the ackee; the National Tree, the blue mahoe; and the National Motto, "Out of Many, One People". Further, there was a national song for schools, "I Pledge My Heart" written by author Vic Reid and sung to the tune of "I Vow to Thee My Country". On October 2, 1961, the public was invited to submit entries for three competitions: one for a flag for independent Jamaica, one for the words of a proposed National Anthem and another for the music for this anthem. Awards of £100 each were offered for the accepted design for the Flag, and for the words and music for the Anthem.

During the months of May and June, the government issued invitations to other governments, mainly members of the Commonwealth; former governors of Jamaica; Sir Arthur Richards (now Lord Milverton), Sir John Huggins and Sir Hugh Foot; ecclesiastical organizations, and international personalities with whom Jamaica had had a special relationship.[1] Outstanding Jamaicans including Keith Johnson, Dr Marcus James, Dr Victor Page and W. A. Domingo who were living abroad, were also invited. Because of other engagements, Harry Belafonte could not attend.

And it was the wish of everyone that Jamaica's favourite member of the Royal family, Princess Margaret, would attend the ceremonies as the representative of her sister, Her Majesty the Queen.[2] After the elections, Sangster became the chairman of the Consultative Committee.[3] Over the years, he had developed a style of administration that involved the delegation of responsibilities to specific people who had special disciplines and a system of meticulous reporting. This was applied during the following four months. Officials in government and members of the planning committees began to know they could expect a telephone call from him at any time to enquire what progress they had made with their assignments.

Although Independence was in early August, up to almost the end of May no decision was taken as to what the National Flag would look like or what the National Anthem would be. Where the flag was concerned the first step taken was on June 6 when a Joint Parliamentary Committee of the House of Representatives agreed to the colours, black, green and gold.[4] The committee also agreed that the flag should consist basically of horizontal stripes, with the colours being arranged so that there would be a centre black band with gold stripes above and below and with outer stripes of green at the top and bottom. Unfortunately, it resembled the flag of Tanganyika.

The new design had a diagonal cross, or saltire, in gold, one-sixth in size of the fly of the flag. The top and bottom triangles created by the cross were green, and the hoist and fly triangles, that is the one nearest the staff and the other at the end of the flag, were black.

Now a third party, the People's Political Party led by an Attorney, Millard Johnson had contested the recent General Elections. His party was a resuscitation of the party that Marcus Garvey had founded years before, and like Garvey's Universal Negro Improvement Association, the colours of his flag were black, green and red.

Johnson preached a philosophy of "black power". His political meetings attracted thousands and frightened elements in Jamaica's upper society as well as some of the leadership in both political parties. His party did not win one seat, but some members of the legislature still remembered the response of the crowds to the black power message Johnson preached. The crowds were large. The crowds included the poor and the dispossessed. And Rastafarians.

Influential sectors of the Jamaican society were afraid at that time of anything black, whether it was black power or skin colour. Black was ugly. Black was dirty. On the other hand, white was pure. White was beautiful. And all this prejudice came out during the debate in the House about the flag.[5]

Sangster moved the motion for the debate and Florizel Glasspole, Leader of Opposition Business in the House, seconded it. Glasspole began by saying there were a number of persons in Jamaica "who are not quite happy about some of the colours that have been chosen because they bear some resemblance to the colours of an organization that is not quite popular in Jamaica today". He was, of course, referring to Millard Johnson's political party, but dismissed it as irrelevant. He said:

> The fact is, members of the committee from both sides of the House sat and spent ceaseless hours to arrive at a design for the flag which will give us the enthusiasm and inspiration that many of us used to have when we were small boys going to school; and when we saw the Union Jack we felt a rather stimulating feeling in our bones.
>
> The colours here have particular significance. I know some would have loved some sort of carry-over from the British flag included in Jamaica's flag but there was very strong feeling on both sides, that the Flag selected should be something new. It does not mean that there is any intention of cutting our association with Britain. It does not mean that we are any less friendly to the United Kingdom.

At this point Bustamante interjected by saying "I thought it would be a good thing to copy something from the British Flag. However, it has not been done and this is a most charming pattern".

The first personal reference of concern about the black in the flag came from Felix Toyloy, member for South Trelawny. "I do not like it. I do not like the black," he said. And when asked by B.B. Coke, why, he said, "it is a sign of distress". Andrew Ross from the constituency of East St Mary also expressed objection to the black. His objection was because of its relationship to the Millard Johnson party. "I saw motor cars flying this type of Flag in my Constituency, and I do not see why we should have a Flag like that."

In the end, however, following support for the Flag by Bustamante, Roy McNeill, Edward Seaga and Norman Manley,

Donald Sangster was able to ask the House to approve unanimously the proposals regarding the flag.

And, at the suggestion of Florizel Glasspole, all the members of the House stood and shouted their approval.

The ayes had it on June 20, 1962.[6]

13 | A NATIONAL ANTHEM

In the meanwhile, progress on the selection of a National Anthem was dragging along wearily. Many entries in response to the government's invitation were received at the Independence Secretariat from poets, scholars, politicians and others, and in January, six months before, they were sent to 12 anonymous persons—who did not know each other. Four entries received the most votes from these 12 persons.

The day after the decision was taken on the National Flag, members of the House of Representatives took a short adjournment to listen to the recording of one of the anthems being considered in the lobby of the House.[1] On the resumption, Sangster invited the House to approve this composition as the National Anthem. He was anxious for a decision to be taken as Independence Day was a mere six weeks away. He pointed out that the Premier Alexander Bustamante, and ministers Seaga, Lightbourne and himself would be leaving Jamaica the following day to spend three weeks in Washington D.C. and London, and if a decision was not taken that day the time between their return and Independence Day would be drastically short.

Sangster felt the national spirit would be hurt and it would be wrong if when the Jamaican flag was hoisted at Independence, Jamaicans had to sing the British National Anthem, "God Save The Queen". "I feel that something else could be found that will be pleasing in words and tune, but if this House can see its way in the peculiar circumstances in which we are placed, to say that this will be used on the 6th of August," he pleaded. "It may not meet your musical feeling but the national aspirations of our people. So, I put it to the House that the Anthem will be approved."

However, members on both sides of the House felt the selected anthem did not stir any feeling of national pride. The recording heard by members was of poor quality. In addition, the musicians, Mapletoft and Allison Poulle, to whom the recording had been sent by Sangster, had not yet modified it. One by one, B.B. Coke, Dr Herbert Eldemire, Keble Munn, Matthew Henry and C.L.A. Stuart, and others in the House objected to it. Edward Seaga was prepared to compromise. "If this is the last chance, then I am prepared to accept what we have heard here tonight as our National Anthem because when August 6 comes I do not intend to stand for any other National Anthem," he said.

Robert Lightbourne, an amateur musician, said the procedure used for the selection was wrong in that the words were written first and then someone was asked to compose the music. "All the famous writers in the world wrote the music and words together. There is no other way," he pronounced. Actually, he was wrong, as many of the great Broadway musicals were a collaboration of lyrics and music written by different persons.

In the end, the House adjourned without a decision being reached. The House was not scheduled to meet until the return to Jamaica of Bustamante, his ministerial team and advisers.

What surprised many was that the reason for the Washington visit was "largely because of the fact that a new Government had taken office in Jamaica and there was need to get acquainted with the American Administration". The implication was that getting acquainted with President John F. Kennedy and the American administration was more important than deciding on an anthem for the new nation-to-be.

So it was off to Washington D.C. for Bustamante to hold discussions with President John F. Kennedy. The result of these talks was that Jamaica's sugar industry secured a permanent quota of about 40,000 tons of sugar annually on the American market at a premium price.[2] Sangster then continued to England with

Bustamante for discussions on defence and economic assistance. But to everyone's surprise, and even Sangster's, an informal private meeting of the House of Representatives was summoned by Speaker of the House Tacius Golding, while the Bustamante-led team which included Sangster was in Washington D.C. At this meeting a National Anthem composed by an Englishman, Bandmaster Wade of the West India Regiment and recorded at the Federal Recording Studio under the supervision of advertising executive Vin Kelly, was selected.[3] The official release issued after the meeting said:

> Consequent on the discussion that took place at the meeting of the House of Representatives on the 21st of June 1962, with reference to the selection of a National Anthem, Members of the House on the invitation of the Honourable Speaker met at Gordon House on Wednesday 27th June 1962 at 2.30 p.m. The meeting was of an informal nature and Members took the opportunity of listening and examining closely the words and music of several prospective anthems. After the most anxious consideration, Members expressed the view that the hoisting of the National Flag ought to be accompanied with the singing of the new National Anthem, and it was unanimously agreed that the Anthem, the words of which are attached, should be selected as the new National Anthem of Jamaica.
>
> The Members felt strongly that a National Anthem should be a source of unity and should have words and music that would prove acceptable to all sections of the community. Members believe that the selection that they have made has all the necessary attributes of a National Anthem, and will wholeheartedly be accepted as such by the people of Jamaica.
>
> The meeting closed with all the members enthusiastically singing this National Anthem—all members standing.
>
> Formal approval of this selection will be moved at the next meeting of the House of Representatives.

The words of the anthem were:

Jamaicans proud we stand today,
Our homeland fair and free.
Against the foe we will defend,
Our liberty.
Our island home, through years to come
Our faith in thee is sure
Jamaicans free, we're proud to be,
Today and evermore.
Our heritage we proudly bear,
From many peoples, One,
This island home we hold
so dear, its praise be sung:
Eternal Father, God of all,
Give us the strength to stand
Steadfast and true to meet the call,
Jamaica is our land.

The first major comment on this decision was by Ulric Simmonds, the powerful political reporter of the *Sunday Gleaner*. "It is a pity that the anthem under consideration— and the words are poor—is one composed by an Englishman and not by a Jamaican of whatever race," he wrote. "And by Englishman, I mean one who is not normally domiciled in Jamaica."[4]

The next public comment came from the barrister-at-law, E.C.L. Parkinson, who was to become speaker of the House five years later. He said:

How has it happened that our National Anthem has not been written by a Jamaican? And what alarms me, too, are the words of this Anthem. The patriotic sentiments they purport to express are in order, but the words are strung together in a clumsy and disconnected manner, and with the most awkward phrasing. These words as they stand will be no credit to us.[5]

G. St C. Scotter, a *Gleaner* columnist said, "it does not seem altogether a satisfactory procedure that the Jamaica National Anthem should be chosen at an informal meeting of members of the House."[6]

Sangster, of course, was livid. On his return to Jamaica he called Golding to his office, reminded him that he was the Leader of the House and that it was he who decided when meetings should be held. In any case, no informal meeting of the House had the authority to take such a momentous decision as that of selecting Jamaica's National Anthem. Golding's comment was that his action was a judgmental one in the interest of ensuring there was a National Anthem in time for Independence. That, Sangster told him, was of no concern to the Speaker; it was for the Government to ensure there was one.

What angered Sangster even more was the competition for an anthem had resulted in words composed by Rev. Hugh Sherlock, a prominent Methodist minister of religion, and music composed by Robert Lightbourne, a minister of government, being chosen. Both had been written independently of each other and as Lightbourne had indicated in the debate this was a difficult way of composing a song.

The Consultative Committee, however, had liked both, and Sangster had instructed Easton Soutar, the deputy clerk of the House to contact Mapletoft Poulle to ask him to try to marry the words and the music chosen. Poulle was a solicitor by profession and a brilliant musician and pianist, and was himself a composer and leader of the orchestra which performed at many of the annual Little Theatre Movement's pantomimes.

Poulle found words and music incompatible. He informed Sangster of his finding and offered to re-write Lightbourne's music to match Sherlock's moving words, and to even modify it in some lines as in their original state the words were not conducive to song form. Sangster agreed. Poulle selected four bars of the 32 bars given to him, and around, and through those, composed a 21-bar Anthem. Simultaneously, Poulle's wife, who was also a competent musician, reconstructed the words and made very minor modifications to fit the new music, while retaining the sense of the original verse. In addition, they added the triumphant coda, "Jamaica, Jamaica, Jamaica, land we love".

All this had taken place unbeknown to the Speaker and members of the House when they chose Brigadier Wade's composition as the national anthem at the Legislature's informal meeting on June 27.

Commenting on the choice made at that meeting, the *Gleaner's* editorial on July 19 noted that:

> We have not heard anyone speak in praise of this anthem. Perhaps it has merits, but from our point of view it has one major demerit. It was not written by someone who has a natural association with the traditions and aspirations of Jamaica and its people. It is to be hoped therefore that at its meeting today the House of Representatives will reverse the informal decision of its members and select a composition authored and arranged by Jamaicans who have been long connected with the traditions, the aspirations and the music of the Jamaican people.
>
> It is very, very important that a nation's symbols should be indigenous. The informal incipient mistake should be rectified.

Interestingly, the *Gleaner's* editorial even noted that there were many Jamaicans:

> ...even opponents of the People's National Party are numbered among them—who would have wished that it could have been possible to select 'Jamaica Arise' (which was the PNP's anthem), as Jamaica's national anthem, for instance, that the PNP would eschew using this song for say ten years and then having the whole country adopt it as Jamaica's national anthem when its memory as a political song had faded.

This, of course, could not, and was not to be.

Later that day, Sangster re-introduced a motion for the House to decide on a national anthem. But before he did, members of both chambers of the Legislature went to the nearby St George's Church where they heard the Wade composition and the joint Sherlock/Lightbourne/Poulle composition, performed by the Jamaica Constabulary Force Orchestra, an organist and singers and conducted by Lloyd Hall, one of Jamaica's prominent musicians.

The choir was magnificent. Some Legislators were moved to tears. This time there was no dissent. There was no doubt that the prayer as contained in the Sherlock-Lightbourne-Poulle anthem was the choice. There was no need for ayes, and members did not as they had done for the Wade anthem, stand and sing it. There was relief in Sangster's voice as he moved for the acceptance of the anthem and closed the debate. He said:

> I beg to close the debate which started on June 21, that the same Anthem which was then put to the House for approval be now finally approved by the House as the National Anthem of Jamaica.

The *Daily Gleaner* in its editorial the following day expressed the national relief of the people at the decision. It said:

> The National Anthem has been finally chosen and the Legislature made its acceptance unanimous. Indeed, members of both political parties represented in the House of Representatives and the Legislative Council have spoken in high praise of the words and music and the Jamaican public in the majority are likely to follow their leaders in this matter.
>
> It is good that they were able to agree on an anthem which will be regarded now, and in the future, as the product of the Jamaican people on the widest possible basis of political agreement. In this respect we cannot agree with Mr Glasspole that it should not be made to appear that preference has been given to a Jamaican composition rather than to an anthem composed by an Englishman temporarily resident in Jamaica.

> We think that the people of Jamaica should be impressed
> with the fact that it is Jamaica's national anthem and take
> pride in it the more because it is the product of their own
> poetry and their own music and their own religious attitudes.
> It is not that we do not consider that an Englishman could
> not write a suitable anthem for Jamaica, but it is better for
> it to be written for Jamaicans by Jamaicans.

To the credit of Poulle and Lightbourne, both men did not accept a fee for their work. Indeed, when Poulle was asked by Theodore Sealy, chairman of the Independence Committee what his charge was, he replied. "I could never charge money for this. It is my service to my country. I only ask that my name and that of my wife be linked with the names of the other composers of the work."

And, in a comment to the *Gleaner*, Lightbourne said: "I was sent a cheque for £500 for being the winner of the competition for the Anthem – a cheque which incidentally I have not cashed as I regarded it as an honour to have been asked to contribute to the making of our National Anthem."

The report in the *Gleaner* announcing the choice of the National Anthem gave sole credit to Lightbourne. Subsequently, however, he agreed to have Mapletoft Poulle's name associated with his as a joint composer of the anthem.[7]

There would be a flag to fly and an anthem to be played and sung when midnight came on August 5 to usher a new day, a new era and a new beginning for the new nation of Jamaica.

Donald Sangster could feel proud.

14 | ON YOUR MARK

The success of the smooth transition into Independence was due to a large extent to the direction of Theodore Sealy who was the chairman of the Independence Celebrations Committee. But it was Sangster's leadership with his meticulous attention to detail, and as the minister with responsibility for the overall organization of the functions and the associated celebrations which gave it a special glory.

After India and Pakistan, which obtained independence from Britain in 1947, Ceylon and Burma in 1948, Sudan in 1956, Ghana in 1957, Nigeria and Cyprus in 1960 and Kuwait, Sierra Leone and Tanzania in 1961, Jamaica became the next in the de-colonization process by Britain to enjoy this status. In addition, Jamaica was one of the smallest countries and with one of the smallest populations in the world to arrive at nationhood.

Jamaicans from across the diaspora came to the island to join their relatives and friends and share the joy. Over 150 journalists attached to newspapers, magazines, and radio and television stations came to tell the world about this little island.[1]

Jamaicans had already made an impact in various fields and disciplines on the world stage. There were Herb McKenley, Arthur Wint, George Rhoden and Les Laing who startled the world at the Helsinki Olympics in 1952 with their record-breaking victory in the 400 metres. There was George Headley, the first batsman to score two centuries in one test match at Lord's in London, the world centre for the sport.

Jamaican coffee, cocoa, bananas, sugar, rum and other products had already given Jamaica's name a special taste on the palates of the connoisseurs of the world. Singers Harry Belafonte,

Willard White and Archie Lewis gave Jamaica a special place in the world of art and entertainment. Authors Vic Reid and Claude McKay were internationally known, and poet Una Marson was a respected broadcaster in England and throughout the Caribbean. Bauxite, one of the useful metals of the 20th century, was discovered in the island.

The journalists were accommodated in Irvine Hall at the University of the West Indies. Sangster and Seaga led the ministers who moved among these journalists, along with officers of the then Government Public Relations Office, to encourage them to tell the stories of yesterday's Jamaica and the now. It was a heady and exciting time for Jamaica.

It was even considered important for Jamaicans to be appropriately dressed for the various ceremonies involving the special independence guests, Her Royal Highness Princess Margaret and the Earl of Snowdon. A document was therefore released by the Independence Celebrations Committee on the types of dress which should be worn.[2] The document covered functions of various kinds, including the welcome ceremony at the Palisadoes Airport, the National Service in the Spanish Town Cathedral, the reception at King's House, the state banquet, the state ball and the state opening of Parliament.

It began by stating that Her Royal Highness The Princess Margaret, did not wish to put anyone to unnecessary expense by buying special clothes.

However, at the official welcome at the Palisadoes Airport and at the civic welcome in Kingston, gentlemen who were to be presented should wear full dress uniform with sword, Orders, decorations and medals (if they were entitled to do so) or morning dress or a lounge suit. Ladies who were to be presented should wear a day dress with hat.

Informal dress could be worn at the youth rally, and at the service in the Spanish Town Cathedral. Gentlemen should wear a lounge suit and ladies a day dress with hat.

At the evening reception at King's House, gentlemen should wear either evening dress (tails and white tie) with Orders, decorations and miniature medals, or service mess kit or a black tie or white dinner jacket or a lounge suit. Ladies should wear an evening dress, long or short.

At the state banquet and at the state ball, gentlemen should wear either evening dress (tails and white tie) with orders, decorations and miniature medals, or service mess kit or a black or white dinner jacket. Ladies should wear an evening dress, long or short.

Gentlemen should wear a dinner jacket or a lounge suit and Ladies should wear an evening dress or afternoon dress without a hat at the national parade, flag raising ceremony and fireworks display. The dress to be worn at the Prime Minister's reception was less formal with gentlemen wearing only a lounge suit and ladies wearing a cocktail dress without a hat.

At the state opening of Parliament, gentlemen were required to wear full dress uniform with sword, orders, decorations and medals (if they were entitled to do so) or morning dress or a lounge suit, while ladies were required to wear a day dress with hat.

At the civic welcome in Montego Bay, gentlemen should wear a lounge suit while ladies should wear an afternoon dress with hat.

Ladies who were to be presented to Her Royal Highness were to wear gloves at all functions. These gloves did not have to be white and they should not be removed before the wearer was presented to Her Royal Highness.

Where presentations were being made to Princess Margaret, the guidelines were that they should approach Her Royal Highness from her right, with husbands in front of wives. Gentlemen should bow and ladies curtsy before shaking hands. However, when they were presented to the Earl of Snowdon, her husband, the gentlemen should not bow and the ladies should not curtsy.

In addition, gentlemen should not bow from the waist or thrust forward their shoulders, but should lower their heads to an almost horizontal position and then raise it. Care should also be taken to look down while bowing. Ladies when curtsying should keep their backs straight and should not bow their heads.

The final advice was that when shaking the hands of the royal couple, as little pressure as possible should be used.

Despite the hint that Princess Margaret did not wish guests attending these events to go to unnecessary expense, classy stores such as Nathan's and Issa's Department Store and Topper on King Street, were deluged with requests for gloves, dress shirts and bow ties. Tailors such as D.B. Dyer and Herman Farel had to employ additional journeymen to cope with orders for dinner jackets and tails. Friends also gathered in homes to rehearse how to bow and curtsy. Some also flew to Miami and New York to find the appropriate dress and accessories.

Oh, yes, Jamaicans certainly knew the importance of being properly attired.

And then after the celebrations were over, the Photographic Departments of the Government Public Relations Department and the *Daily Gleaner* were crowded with the ladies and gentlemen who were guests at these functions purchasing photographs of their presence with royalty to send to relatives and friends abroad and to place in their photo albums.

Meanwhile, the state of New York gave official recognition to plans being made by the Jamaican community there to celebrate the occasion of independence. In a special proclamation from the governor's office in Albany, Governor Nelson A. Rockefeller proclaimed the period August 5 to 11 as "Jamaica Independence Week." The proclamation said:

> On August 6, 1962, the people of the beautiful neighbouring
> island of Jamaica will enjoy a new status. On that day they

become citizens of an independent country, a member of the Commonwealth of Nations.

Many thousand men and women in the Empire State are of Jamaican origin. They are, incidentally, valued and valuable fellow citizens. To them, the peaceful attainment of Jamaican independence and membership in the Commonwealth of Nations is a great event, the culmination of years of endeavour.

It is fitting and neighbourly that the rest of us sympathise with this sentiment and co-operate in celebrating the occasion.

NOW, THEREFORE, I, Nelson A. Rockefeller, governor of the State of New York, do hereby proclaim the period August 5 to August 11, 1962, to be "Jamaica Independence Week".[3]

And as Jamaicans do, wherever they are, they celebrated day and night.

The euphoria of the independence celebrations had barely subsided when Jamaica hosted the Ninth Central American and Caribbean Games at the new National Stadium beginning on August 11 and ending on August 25. Two weeks later there was another pleasure. Prime Minister Bustamante and Gladys Longbridge, his private secretary of over 20 years, were married. Sangster gave the bride away. Shearer was Bustamante's bestman.

It was a family affair; Shearer and Sangster were kinsmen of the groom.[4]

After the celebrations and festivities of Independence, the national joy of the marital culmination of the Bustamante/ Longbridge 20-year long love affair, and the pride of seeing the Jamaican Flag unfurled among the flutter of flags of the world at the United Nations, it became time to concentrate on the work of building the Jamaica that Jamaicans expected.

This work had already started. Sangster had presented a budget for the year 1962 to 1963 in May, just one month after winning the general elections. The previous PNP Government had prepared a wait-and-see budget, which was really a bookkeeping exercise of balancing the books pending the election decision. Government's annual budgets are usually presented in April each year but the holding of elections in April had not given Sangster time to do more than cosmetic changes to the PNP Government's draft.

The Throne Speech which preceded the laying of the expenditure budget indicated it would be a "holding Budget" designed to continue the existing programmes and projects while the government proceeded to re-assess the merits of the programmes, determine to what extent they should be modified and run down or eliminated altogether, or approved and carried on, while the government formulated its own development programme. And while the process of formulating the new development programmes was being attended, the majority of the existing programmes in housing, agriculture, education and other fields would be maintained.[5]

The expenditure budget was presented during the last week of May,[6] and then it was "joy of joy" when, in presenting the revenue budget during the last week of July, Sangster announced there would be no increased taxation that year.[7] Revenue to be collected, he said, amounted to £30.4 million. In addition, loans amounting to £4.2 million would be raised to help cover the total expenditure of £45.2 million. He said the government had already raised an exchequer loan from Britain of just over £1 million and it was intended to raise £3 million in loans in Washington and London between September and October. And, to prepare the legal authority for obtaining the loans needed for development, he presented a Bill seeking the authority of the House of Representatives to increase the government's loan power from £12 million to £25 million.

Later when he presented the supplementary budget on October 30, he pointed out that the government had not yet, even then, fully examined the state of the economy.[8] The *Daily Gleaner* saw it as a half-way-house on the road to the budget for 1963-64 which had to be "comprehensive, definite and dynamic". It provided for new taxation in a small number of areas and a relief of taxation in others, resulting in additional expenditure of £6.3 million, and bringing total expenditure in the year to £49 million. The year before budgeted expenditure was £4 million less.

Stamp duties on cheques were increased from two-pence to three-pence with effect from the following January to bring in £25,000 in a full year; stamp duty on conveyances were increased from seven shillings and six pence (7/6d) per £50 to ten shillings (10/-) per £50 in respect of property over £500 in value with the present surcharge of 25 percent remaining to bring in a further £25,000 in a full year; those who imported wooden furniture were to pay higher customs duties, the preference rates increased from 20 percent to 30 percent, and the general rate from 25 percent to 35 percent, and the customs tariffs on imported metal furniture to be increased by 10 percent to bring in £100,000 in a full year; a surtax on motor car imports increased from 5 percent to 10 percent so that the effective rate of duty would be 30 percent preferential and 50 percent general to bring in a further £100,000 in a full year; an increase of one penny (1d) per gallon on gasoline to bring in a further £100,000 in a full year; local beer was increased by one penny (1d) per bottle and imported beer by two pence (2d) per bottle to bring in a further £220,000 in a full year.

To please a waiting nation, there were some tax cuts. For instance, truck licences were to be reduced from next year by 50 percent where the trucks were to be engaged in transporting people and goods to markets; a reduction of 25 percent in market fees to aid market vendors; the removal of the two shillings and six pence (2/6d) withholding tax levied on money brought into the island for buildings and utilities to provide incentives in these sectors; building societies were to be relieved of tax on reserves up to 7½ percent of reserves, and building societies and mortgages to be relieved of stamp duties on values below £1,500, from the previous £500; and the joint earned income of husbands and wives up to a total of £1,500 to be separated.

Sangster's comment was that the new measures reflected the first six months thinking of the new government. He described them as directed to stimulating local production, revitalizing the economy and providing immediate employment. He promised a fuller presentation "next time" in the following year's budget.

Meanwhile, Sir Kenneth Blackburne, the last of the British governors of Jamaica had been granted the courtesy of remaining for three months as governor-general following independence. Because of the time limit of his appointment, there was speculation by political pundits and wishful thinking by "wanna-be" successors in his party and government that Bustamante would resign as prime minister. After all he had said many times before that he would be the first native governor of Jamaica—and the post of governor-general was even much more prestigious. Wily as he was, Bustamante delayed the announcement of Blackburne's successor as long as possible.

Then Bustamante assigned Vale Royal to Donald Sangster in his capacity as minister of finance. This had been the official residence of former colonial secretaries who in pre-independence Jamaica were second only to the governor in the administration of the island. This was his signal that he regarded Sangster as his chief lieutenant. Then, and only then, did he formally announce that he would not relinquish the office of prime minister, and that the president of the Senate, Clifford Campbell, would be the new governor-general.[9] He also announced that a new official residence would be built for the prime minister. In due course this was built on Hope Road in St Andrew adjacent to King's House, the official residence of the governor-general.

Campbell's appointment further firmed up the status of

Sangster. With Bustamante remaining as prime minister there was no purpose for Lightbourne to continue his struggle for succession to the post. Indeed it was seen as a master-stroke by Bustamante as with immediate political ambition denied, the divisions which were being created in the Cabinet were put aside, albeit temporarily.

The assignment of Vale Royal to Sangster as his official residence was a stick in the throat of Norman Manley and the People's National Party. In planning for independence, Manley had chosen this rambling colonial-type two-storey house to be the official residence of the prime ministers of Jamaica. It sat on four acres of landscaped lands in central St Andrew, a quick-drive distance from King's House. Its broad verandah wrapped around the house on three sides. From the top floor there was a sweeping view of lower St Andrew stretching as far as Kingston Harbour. Behind it were the lower hills of the Blue Mountain range, not yet then scattered with houses.

The property on which it stood was much smaller than when it was an estate known as Prospect Pen owned by Simon Taylor, an English planter. He owned four other estates and more than 2,000 slaves. The house was built at the end of the 17th century. One of its interesting features was a lookout tower on the roof from which could be seen ships as they sailed into Kingston Harbour.

Manley believed he would have won the pre-Independence elections. The building and land space was reminiscent of his own home, Drumblair set on 30 acres of land one mile to the north of Vale Royal which he had purchased from one Alice Raney in 1936 for £1,500. He had lived there ever since. Along with his wife, the sculptor Edna Manley, he had turned Drumblair into the social and cultural centre for Jamaican artists, writers, sculptors, actors and actresses. A fact that was not then publicly known, was that Manley had mortgaged the property to fund the expenses of the PNP, and win or lose the pre-independence elections he would have had to sell it.

In rejecting Manley's plan to have Vale Royal the designated official residence of the prime minister, Bustamante said that as far as he was concerned wherever he lived was the prime minister's official residence:

> I now live in my own home of five large bedrooms," he said.
> "I will not live in Vale Royal with one bedroom and two coops.
> The previous Government decided that Vale Royal was good
> enough for any ordinary Prime Minister, but I am not an
> ordinary Prime Minister; I am an outstanding Prime Minister.

He even mischievously suggested the use of Vale Royal as a maternity home.[10]

After a stormy debate about the appropriateness of assigning the house to Sangster, with members calling others "stinking fool", "stinking liar" and other epithets, the House of Representatives approved a motion moved by Edwin Allen for the use of Vale Royal as a residence for the minister of finance or for any other purpose the government might decide.

15 | STEPPING UP THE LADDER

Four months later, on March 11, 1963 just before the end of the first year in office as government, Bustamante appointed Sangster as deputy prime minister.[1]

Bustamante was 79 years old. He was slowing down. He had no intention of retiring as yet, but recognised he had to shed some of his responsibilities. True, no such office was provided for in the constitution, but it plugged an administrative hole in the structure of government.

In creating this post, Bustamante chose to retain those functions which enjoyed the pleasures of protocol. These included receiving courtesy calls from visiting heads of state and government and diplomats. He also loved to host potential investors when he regaled them with stories of his journeys as a young man in Spain and other countries, including how he invested in the New York Stock Exchange and wisely sold his shares just before the crash of 1929.

And, by still holding the office of prime minister with its power he also enjoyed the homage paid by his party and union officials without having to carry out the day-to-day functions of leader.

In appointing Sangster as his deputy, Bustamante also achieved three other major objectives. First, it settled an internecine wrangle for party leadership and consequently his successor as prime minister should he step down. Secondly, it established an office to fill an administrative gap within which Sangster himself had been functioning since the party was returned to office; and it also awarded Sangster for distinguished service, both to party and country, particularly since Independence.

Indeed, Sangster had been a member of the House of Representatives since 1949, longer than many of his Cabinet colleagues; he had held ministerial posts—Social Welfare and Finance in previous governments and was currently minister of finance and leader of the House. Since Independence he had spearheaded the new nation's financing programme, raising nearly £5 million loan funds in the United States of America, the United Kingdom, and Jamaica, had gained convertibility for Jamaica's currency through membership in international monetary organizations, and by his statesmanlike conduct of affairs "inspired hope and confidence at home and abroad" according to the editors of *Spotlight* magazine.

Sangster took to his new office like a racehorse tethered for weeks, then suddenly let loose in an open pasture. Observers saw new pep in his step. He was now the undisputed deputy leader of the party as well as of his colleagues in the Cabinet. He seemed more relaxed and more confident than he had been in recent months.

His first major task in the cloak of Deputy Prime Minister was his presentation of the government's first real budget since its election one year earlier. This budget presentation was on April 10, 1963. The elections were won on April 10, 1962, and the anniversary coincidence, Sangster noted, was a good omen for the future.[2]

His colleague Edward Seaga, the Minister of Development and Welfare who had already been identified as the Jamaica Labour Party's most creative thinker and visionary, had already propounded a formula for an outstanding socio-economic problem— overcrowding in the capital Kingston and under-development in the country:

> While other countries are moving with the trend to provide more employment in the cities, we have learned that we must not move with the trend, but against it. We must create more employment on the land to check the migration from rural areas to the city.

This was obviously government policy, for in the 1963-64 budget there was an overwhelming concentration of promised activity in the rural areas, and this was reflective of an early cabinet declaration that "to the PNP Government, Kingston had become Jamaica; rural life must be rehabilitated".

So, according to Governor-General Sir Clifford Campbell, in his first Throne Speech, there would be an attack on unemployment where hardship strikes most– in rural Jamaica. There would be an emphasis on construction – housing, roads and water supplies—as a means of providing the largest number of jobs. "The Government," he said, "hopes that provision of these important amenities will render the rural areas in which they are provided more attractive to our rural population."

There was a new programme for agriculture, designed to give farmers greater security and to make use of land resources. A Statutory Marketing Board would be an integral part of this new programme.

There would be new incentive legislation for industrial expansion, with emphasis on processing and export marketing in rural areas. There was to be a factory building programme to be handled through the Development Finance Corporation with emphasis on placing factories in country parishes. Manufacturers siting factories in rural parishes would get an extra tax-free holiday from one to ten years over and above the basic ten years.

It was with the revenue budget that Sangster earned high credits from the private sector and analysts. Jamaica's public debt, which was £45.4 million at the end of the financial year 1962/63, would climb to £51 million at the end of the 1963/64 financial year. This would lessen the need for the imposition of higher taxation.

Sangster explained:

> In the search for additional taxation we have sought not to restrict development but to give additional encouragement to protect local industries and to give more incentives. We have

sought to avoid taxation on necessary items, and to make
some services, postal, for example, more self-supporting.
We are trying to institute a policy line which will lead to
reduction of the island's dependence on imports. The whole
emphasis is going to be on local production to provide more
jobs.[3]

Increased import duties and surtax were tagged on to luxury
and semi-luxury items, chiefly whisky (an estimated consumption
of 81,000 gallons), gin (estimated consumption 14,035) and
brandy (estimated consumption 10, 205 gallons), air conditioning
equipment, refrigerators and jewelry. And to aid local industries in
some cases and force increased production in others, import duties
also went up on such items as hams, tinned soups and juices, sugar
confectionery, and coffee extracts. In instances, i.e. cigarettes and
footwear, where increased excise duties were imposed, the rates
were still highly in favour of the local products, compared to higher
impositions on foreign supplies.

Sangster also announced that the Government had discussed
with commercial banks the question of extending credit for the
agricultural sector and long-term credit for the private sector. Bank
loans had fallen by £1.7 million the previous year, while deposits
had increased by £6.7 million. Clearly, the volume of savings was
not being productively used, and the problem of how to carry these
savings into productive enterprises was being studied. One solution,
he felt, might be a change to "corporate concept" of the country's
financial structure – the breaking down of personal ownership of
companies and industries to corporate ownership by the building
up of a stock market in which shares would be freely exchanged.

For some time, we will need external investments, but it is
clear that the ultimate goal must be increasing participation
by local people in all aspects of Jamaica's economic
development. This is going to become more and more possible

as standards of living increase, and those enjoying higher standards will owe a duty to the country to put aside some of their earnings for investment towards development.

In commenting on the budget, the *Daily Gleaner's* editorial pointed to:

> The concentration of funds on rural housing, water supplies, farm development and agricultural marketing and the general raising of the capital development programme from £11.6 million last year to £13.5 million this year should produce a much needed revitalization of rural economy. To this must be added the money to be spent on roads on land settlements, on housing estates and as feeders to the main communications system of the island.
>
> The focal point of the Budget appears to be housing which has been raised from £500,000 last year to some £2.2 million this year, and the Deputy Prime Minister said that most of this is to be concentrated in the rural areas. That is good. While some progress, however small, has been made in housing in urban areas, the countryside is still shabby and prehistoric, and many villages are dismal and desolate in appearance.
>
> We note, too, that in addition to this emphasis on rural housing, the Minister has announced a plan for the expansion of cottage craft and the institution of government efforts for the sale of the products of that craft to augment the agricultural revenues of the rural people.[4]

This craft development programme was to be implemented by Edward Seaga's Ministry of Development and Welfare, but it had been given Sangster's financial blessing because of his own long interest in craft production in his birth parish of St Elizabeth. There, in almost every household, there was a family member involved in straw craft, embroidery, needlecraft and other cottage production.

The budget had also made provision for the re-organization of the tourism product and the marketing of tourism, and Sangster had long seen that tourism would benefit from a vibrant craft industry.

In addition, the launching of a national airline for Jamaica was imminent. This took place on May 1, 1965, a few months later than was envisaged.

The editorial also noted that "the budget which Mr Sangster announced yesterday is frankly a rural Budget and we do not think that anything less could have been expected from a government which won its position through rural votes".[5]

Promises made. Promises kept.

During the remainder of 1963, Bustamante was relatively active but it was observed that Sangster was close, at his side, in all his public activities. He accompanied Bustamante to the first Conference of Heads of Caribbean Commonwealth Countries in Trinidad & Tobago. The announcement by Bustamante that despite the break-up of the Federation caused by Jamaica, the government would continue to be associated with the regional services, including the University of the West Indies and the Regional Shipping Services, was seen as influenced by Sangster, who as Minister of Finance was a member of the University Council.

The Jamaica Cricket Board had decided to remain in the West Indies cricket team, and this was also believed to have been influenced by Sangster and Norman Manley. Sangster had also accompanied Bustamante to Washington, D.C. for discussions with President John F. Kennedy and his administration. Later that year, too, Jamaica was accepted as a member of the Latin American group in the United Nations, and as a member of the United Nations Economic Commission for Latin America. Exploratory talks also began regarding Jamaica's entry into the Organization of American States. More than any other member of the Bustamante Cabinet, Sangster was seen to have an international outlook on economic, social and cultural affairs, and these decisions seemed to have been influenced by him.

All in all, the year 1963 was a good year for Jamaica. The first woman, Muriel Carnegie,[6] was appointed to act as Custos Rotulorum for the parish of Westmoreland; it was the beginning of a movement in which women in Jamaica began to hold high offices as ambassadors, high commissioners, as financial and permanent secretaries of ministries, heads of government departments and statutory boards. Women were also elected to prestigious national associations and organizations such as Chambers of Commerce, the Private Sector Organization of Jamaica, the Jamaica Manufacturers' Association and the Jamaica Exporters' Association, a trend culminating more recently with the election of women as presidents of our political parties and the prime ministership of Jamaica.

Later that year, a Jamaican young woman, Carol Joan Crawford won the prestigious "Miss World" crown from 39 contestants in London.[7] Sangster, who was a keen beauty contest fan, could hardly contain his joy. He approved funds for printing postage stamps to commemorate her victory.

And the year ended with the United Nations accepting a Jamaican resolution by Cabinet member, Hugh Shearer, that 1968 should be observed as the International Year of Human Rights.[8] Shearer was a senator and minister without portfolio with special responsibilities for external affairs, and in that capacity he was Jamaica's official spokesman at the United Nations from 1962 to 1966.

16 | CHANGING THE GUARD

The signal that an era was coming to an end was seen at the ceremonial opening of Parliament on April 2, 1964. Absent was the tall, dignified figure of Bustamante, attired in his tails and top hat, striding with military gait on Duke Street in Kingston from the offices of the BITU to the Legislative Chambers ahead of the Jamaica Labour Party parliamentarians. It was the first time since 1944 that Sir Alexander was absent on this annual occasion. But his doctors were firm. He needed rest and was ordered to remain in bed. In his place, Donald Sangster led the JLP Senators and Members of Parliament to Gordon House.[1]

Two weeks later Bustamante was operated on at the Walter Reed Hospital in Washington D.C. to remove a cataract from his eye. He was away from Jamaica for about one month and during that time Sangster was appointed acting prime minister.[2]

Bustamante was therefore not present when Sangster presented a £63.9 million budget to Parliament, a staggering £8 million more than the preceding year.[3] The size of the budget led to fears and alarmist rumours of a huge hike in taxes. So there was a national sigh of relief when Sangster subsequently presented the estimates of revenue which revealed that the doleful prophecies of heavy additional taxation to meet the expenditure estimates were not to be fulfilled.

The estimates of revenue were £43.8 million recurrent revenue, £1.7 million capital revenue and total loan receipts £11.7 million. The anticipated deficit was therefore £2.2 million, and new taxes to meet this were expected to realise £1.5 million. And the pleasant fact was that Sangster not only refrained from imposing new taxes to meet the full amount of the anticipated deficit, but also in the manner in which the new taxes were levied so as to cause the least burden on taxpayers, especially the poorer people. There were therefore no increases on the most common articles of food consumed by the poorer classes such as rice, flour, codfish, mackerel, or on widely used fabrics such as khaki and calico.

Instead, the higher taxes were on luxury and semi-luxury goods. Sangster was at pains to point out that the increases were not on the value of the goods, but on existing rates of duty, thus lightening the new imposts to a considerable extent.

On Bustamante's return, he resumed office but worked at a very slow pace. By January 1965, however, he had to once again relinquish his duties to Sangster and asked the Governor-General to appoint him, Sangster, as acting prime minister, acting minister of external affairs and acting minister of defence.

Bustamante continued to live at Jamaica House, the official residence of the Prime Minister, and for the next three years was Prime Minister, de jure. The arrangement was that Sangster carried out the day-to-day duties and responsibilities of Bustamante's previous ministerial offices but that he had to consult with Bustamante who was reluctant to give up the pleasures and prestige of high office. So, Bustamante held court at his official residence every day to members of the Cabinet and officers of the Jamaica Labour Party and the Bustamante Industrial Trade Union who visited him constantly to court his favour and also backbite Sangster.

In his new capacity as acting prime minister, Sangster led Jamaica's delegation to the Commonwealth Prime Minister's Conference in London in July. At this meeting he persuaded the presidents and prime ministers attending of his conviction of the importance of the Commonwealth Parliamentary Association. His intervention led the British Government to increase its financial contribution to the association which had already established its headquarters in London.

He also had the opportunity to speak on Jamaica's attitude to South Africa and Southern Rhodesia's apartheid and Australian migration policies when newspaper reporters from these countries raised these issues with him at a news conference. On the question of migration, he told them that Jamaica believed firmly that this should be reasonably free and certainly should not be based on race; and if this could be considered a criticism of Australia's policies then Jamaica would be prepared to stand by its position. On apartheid and South Africa, he reminded them that even before independence, Jamaica had imposed a boycott of South African goods, and it was now a question of whether there could be collective Commonwealth action to back up Jamaica's unilateral action.

The most controversial item on the agenda of this conference was the escalating racial violence between Africans and Indians taking place in British Guiana and on this issue Jamaica and Trinidad & Tobago were poles apart.[4] Prime Minister Eric Williams of Trinidad & Tobago presented a plan to resolve it which in his view was "the only reasonable way out of the dilemma". His proposals called for:

> A Commonwealth Commission under the supervision of the United Nations, to assume Government responsibility in the country. The Commissioner, to be appointed from a Commonwealth nation and with staff appropriately selected and responsible to the U.N., would have full powers over police, defence forces, electoral machinery, and the civil service;
>
> The Commissioner's first task would be to disarm the population and create a new climate of mutual trust among the people;
>
> The establishment of a Constituent Assembly consisting of all the reputable civic organizations in the country which would agree to safeguard the constitution...

The Williams Plan ruled out an African or Asian as

commissioner as he might take partisan action for either the African or Asian communities in the country. In fact, it regarded only one Commonwealth country, New Zealand, as entirely neutral and fitting his specification.

The British Government's view was that it could not relinquish sovereign rights over the country until the colony was guided to independence. This view was echoed by Sangster:

> The only way to ensure independence in the British-protected territory was for its politicians to work out a rational and practical approach to the racial, social and economic problems which threaten to throw the country into chaos.

Sangster saw no radical and immediate solution to the problem, and that "it is a slow and uphill grind". He stressed that Britain could not avoid its responsibilities for the colony.

Williams' proposals were cold-shouldered at the Conference, not because they lacked merit, but for the main reason that they would cut across the policy of the African prime ministers, that it was the responsibility of the British Government to solve the racial problem and question of independence in Southern Rhodesia. They would have had to back-track on this view, to support joint Commonwealth-United Nations action in British Guiana.

The communiqué issued at the end of the conference justified Sangster's approach. It said:

> The responsibility and authority for leading her remaining colonies to independence must continue to rest with Britain. While several different views were expressed on the methods to be employed, a number of the Prime Ministers expressed the hope that the political leaders of British Guiana would seek urgently a basis for collaboration in the interest of their fellowmen of all races in order to restore mutual confidence among the races and to strengthen a spirit of national purpose and unity. Only in such circumstances could British Guiana hope to sustain true independence.[5]

Two months later, Sangster was again playing a lead role in international issues. This time, it was at the Annual Meeting of the World Bank in Washington D.C. Based on his two years of seeking international industrial investment funds and the increasing competition from more and more independent countries seeking the same funds, he foresaw the need for the co-ordination of an international policy to avoid serious problems in the future.[6]

He pointed out that there was, for example, a pointless competition in the granting of incentives among many developing countries which would soon nullify the benefits to be derived from private capital investment. There was, he said, extravagant tax-free periods, ranging from 15 to 25 years, which some governments had been obliged to grant investors. And, he suggested that the Fund and Bank should take the initiative in developing a policy of rationalizing investment incentives. One country, he pointed out, could not take this action unilaterally unless its competitors were prepared to agree to an acceptable policy.

Locally, he had presented a £30 million Five Year Development Programme to the House of Representatives on October 21, 1964.[7] Sixteen months in the drafting, the programme, with major emphasis on agricultural development to the extent of over £13 million, was based on the recommendations of a World Bank Mission which had visited Jamaica in 1962. It was geared to be spread over the years 1965-66 to 1969-70.

Sources of financing would be Colonial Development and Welfare, a British funding organization, to the extent of £8.4 million, general revenue £2.6 million and loans totaling £18.9 million. Other sectors to benefit from the programme were public health £4.9 million, communications £7.1 million, industrial and trade development £1.5 million and research £195,000. The sum allocated under agriculture provided funding for subsidies to farmers, loans to farmers, state projects and enterprises, land settlements, land improvements, farm water supplies, fisheries and agricultural education. The education aspect of the programme included funding for continuing the existing school building programme to provide a total annual addition of 7,500 places and a net addition of 3,000 places annually. Technical high schools would also be set up outside of Kingston.

Provision was also made for constructing three health centres and improved hospital services. There was also a provision of £1.5 million for government buildings including a new Parliament building, a project dear to Sangster's heart.

Princess Alice Countess of Athlone and Chancellor of the University of the West Indies gets the full attention of Donald Sangster during her 1960 visit to Jamaica.

©The Gleaner Company

Prime Minister Bustamante (far left) and members of his Cabinet observe while Donald Sangster (centre) briefs Princess Margaret on the details of an upcoming state dinner.

Courtesy Hartley Neita

17 | THE WORLD COMES VISITING

Before Jamaica became an independent nation in 1962, official contact with the outside world was limited mainly to England, the United States of America and Canada. There was also limited individual contact with Costa Rica, Panama and Cuba through migration of workers to those countries, and with China and India through migration of indentured workers from those countries. Jamaica also traded with New Zealand, Hong Kong, and there were students from Venezuela who came to schools in Jamaica to study.

Over time, Jamaica had enjoyed official and state visits from the British Royal family. The first was Prince George, who later became King George V. He opened the International Industrial Exhibition in 1891. In later years, Her Majesty Queen Elizabeth II and her husband the Duke of Edinburgh and their children, and Her Royal Highness the Princess Margaret and her husband Lord Snowdon, the Princess Alice, Countess of Athlone and Her Majesty the Queen Mother, and other members of the British Royal family paid several visits to the island.

Other important visitors to Jamaica had included Eleanor Roosevelt, the wife of US President Franklyn Roosevelt; General Paul Magloire, president of Haiti; British Prime Minister Harold Macmillan; Governor of Puerto Rico Luis Muñoz Marín; and US Vice President Charles Dawes.

President Franklyn D. Roosevelt also visited Jamaica in 1940 but did not land. Along with Sir Arthur Richards, the governor of Jamaica who joined him on board his ship, he sailed along the south coast to Portland Bight in Clarendon where he had a long-range view of the site of the US Air and Naval Base which was to be built. This was subsequently named Vernamfield. The only head of state from an African country to visit Jamaica up to then was President William Tubman of Liberia.

Princess Margaret, Paul Magloire, and Muñoz Marín, visited in 1955 when Jamaica celebrated the 300th anniversary of Jamaica's association with Britain. Princess Margaret spent five days during which she opened a new hospital at Morant Bay in St Thomas which was named for her. Muñoz Marín opened the annual Jamaica Agriculture Society's agricultural fair at Denbigh in Clarendon. These visits had been planned by Sangster before he demitted office. Indeed, although the idea of the Tercentenary was a JLP one, it was to the PNP's credit that they carried through the celebrations. In the end, Jamaica 300 turned out to be a year of community celebrations of artistic and athletic events of all kinds and, in hindsight, helped to instill a growing nationalism among the Jamaican people.

With independence, Jamaica became a member of the international family of nations. Our leaders were sitting with and talking to presidents, prime ministers, the heads of international financial and cultural institutions, and ministers of government and their officials at the United Nations and other fora. Jamaica was now free to align itself with any nation or group of nations. In 1955, for example, the invitations to Princess Margaret, General Magloire, and Señor Muñoz Marín were made by the governor through the British Government who was responsible for Jamaica's external affairs. Now, as an independent nation, the Jamaican Government could invite representatives of the world's nations to agree to observe an International Year of Human Rights, which they did in 1968. For the first time, too, the Jamaican Government could invite who it wished to visit the country without having to obtain the permission of its colonial masters in London.

For the first time, Jamaica could also host international conferences of any nature. So, two years after independence,

Sangster invited the Commonwealth Parliamentary Association to hold its 1964 meeting in Jamaica. Jamaica was then one of the most recent countries to achieve nationhood; it was also one of the smallest countries, and least populated, in the Commonwealth. Nevertheless, the invitation was accepted. This was seen as testimony to the respect leaders in these countries had for Sangster. He had been attending meetings of the association from as far back as 1950 in New Zealand, and Barbados, London, Ceylon, Malaya and Canada and had been a positive voice on issues which came to the attention of the association.

Delegates from the widely scattered Commonwealth, known once upon a time as the British Empire, converged on Jamaica. The 127 delegates who came from as close as Barbados, as centrally sited as Great Britain, and as far away as Malaya and Australia, represented peoples who formed a quarter of the world's population of lands that covered a fifth of the globe.[1]

Before the Conference started, delegates were taken on tours of schools, sugar cane plantations, factories, the Chestervale Youth Camp, the Yallahs Valley and housing estates. The visitors lisped a mixture of languages, yet all spoke English. The exotic robes of the African delegates and be-fezzed heads of other Easterners excited the attention of Jamaicans everywhere. Jamaicans were meeting at close hand, people they had previously seen only in the movies, in books, newspapers and magazines, and on television which had been brought to Jamaica only one year before.

Delegates were also the guests of Sangster at a reception held at Vale Royal which allowed them to meet Jamaican officials in the civil service, businessmen and women and social workers.[2] Feature of the night was an all-Jamaican cabaret which had become a highlight of receptions held at Vale Royal. Artistes who performed were Carlos Malcolm and the Afro-Jamaican Rhythms, dancers from the Alma Mock Yen Dance Group of Harbour View with Veneta Salmon as soloist, the Frats Quintet, Lord Creator, the Skates, a young dance team, Lord Jellicoe, comedian Alston Bair, the Blues Busters and Count Ossie and his drums. Adrian Robinson was the master of ceremonies. Among the guests were Carol Joan Crawford, the reigning Miss World, and the reigning Miss Jamaica, Mitzie Constantine.

Delegates also participated in seminars about Jamaica's economic, social and cultural programmes. These were led by Don Mills, the director of the Central Planning Unit, Gloria Scott, an economist, and V.C. Smith, permanent secretary, Ministry of Trade and Industry. Programmes of entertainment included a special performance of the previous year's annual Pantomime, "Queenie's Daughter". The pantomime had been on ice since April after a record run of 51 performances. Comedian Ranny Williams ad libbed with a reference to the presence of the delegates and drew their laughter when he took a pot shot at them with the line, "join the C.P.A. and see the world for free". They were also treated to a performance by the National Dance Theatre Company of Jamaica.

Delegates attended the enshrinement of the body of Marcus Garvey at the King George VI Memorial Park, since re-named National Heroes Park.[3] His body was brought home to Jamaica from the Kendal Green cemetery in London, England, where he had been buried on his death in June 1940.

In 1964, it seemed, the world was in Jamaica.

In welcoming delegates to the Commonwealth Parliamentary Association Conference, Bustamante said: "As long as you are here, this is your home. That is exactly what I mean. This is your home." And Norman Manley in lauding the Commonwealth observed:

It is a living example of the idea of the brotherhood of man, and perhaps one day in the world that supreme idea with the help of the Commonwealth will mount and grow like waves which roll on the cliffs that form barriers of prejudice and distrust among nations, and bring those barriers tumbling down.

Sangster had been deeply involved in the association's activities for many years and was one of its keenest supporters. A history of the association published by the Commonwealth Secretariat, noted that as chairman of the Conference "he was outstanding for his tact, fairness and sincerity, and for his ability to defuse situations which seemed about to erupt. The fact that the 1964 conference was so successful was due in large part to his contribution as Chairman and host".[4]

A problem which almost broke up the Conference was the presence of delegates from Southern Rhodesia. This country was a colony of Britain, but had a constitution which denied the predominantly Black population the right to vote.

Just before the conference began, the president of the Senate of Kenya, Senator T.M. Chokwee told delegates that his delegation was embarrassed by the presence of these delegates from Southern Rhodesia, a country he said which refused to honour the ideals of the CPA. He demanded that these delegates withdraw and unless there was a special reason why they should remain, then the Kenyan delegation would be forced to reconsider its position. The Attorney General of Uganda G.L. Binaisa immediately gave his support to Kenya's position; the Southern Rhodesian government was, he said, defying the British government and all members of the Commonwealth. Other countries, he noted, particularly Jamaica and those of Eastern and Central Asia had shown the world that many races could live together in one country, enjoying the same rights and owning the same duties.

Councillors from Tanzania, Zambia, Ghana, Nigeria, Ceylon, Sierra Leone, Pakistan, Malaysia and India all spoke in support of the withdrawal of the Southern Rhodesian delegation from the conference.

The only counter view was expressed by the New Zealand councillor, J.H. George, who pointed out that the Southern Rhodesian Parliament had been elected in accordance with the constitution which had been conferred by the United Kingdom. Consequently, he said, the delegation was entitled to be present under the constitution of the CPA and should remain.

The discussion lasted two hours. The Afro-Asian Councillors presented their case strongly, but with dignity and restraint. And it was then that Sangster drew on his legal training and parliamentary experience which was far more than most, if not all, the delegates.

The CPA Conference, he pointed out, had no jurisdiction over the internal affairs of any other country. He had led Jamaica's delegation to the Commonwealth Prime Ministers' meeting in London the previous year, and that meeting he said had accepted this position. Further, he emphasised that all delegates now attending this conference of the CPA must be presumed to believe in the rule of law and adherence to the constitution. He read the relevant clauses of the association's constitution under which it was clear that the Southern Rhodesian branch of the association was entitled to send a delegation. He could not, therefore, accept the desire of the Afro-Asian delegates, but he felt that the discussion that the council had had, would, he hoped, achieve the result intended, namely, to let the Southern Rhodesian representatives know that nobody on the council accepted the principle of minority government.

The issue did not end there. It surfaced during a subsequent meeting of the council, and Sangster had to draw on his legal and debating skills again to reduce the temperature of what were often heated interventions. It was Florizel Glasspole, the PNP's delegate on the Jamaican team whose suggestion of a compromise seemed to find favour with the delegates. He pointed out that, according to the Association's constitution, the Southern Rhodesia branch had an unanswerable case to remain and participate in the deliberations. However, the council could not consider the matter solely in terms of the constitution. So he urged the council to defer its decision for 12 months, as had been suggested by G.L. Binaisa of Uganda and to accept that the branch would continue for the present with the status of an affiliated branch.

Feeling that the meeting was nearing a consensus, Sangster argued persuasively for acceptance of Glasspole's compromise solution. If this was agreed to, the conference would continue without any rifts. One by one, he received support from the delegates and the compromise proposal was accepted.

Yet, although the issue of the presence of a Southern Rhodesian delegation at the CPA's conference was settled, there were two demonstrations by students of the University of the West Indies when the conference officially opened. One demonstration was mounted by undergraduates of the university who carried large placards denouncing the racist policies of the Southern Rhodesia government. They placed themselves directly in front of the Assembly Hall where the conference was being held and kept chanting "Freedom" or "Uhuru" depending on whether the delegate arriving was a European or an African or Asian.[5]

The second demonstration was a two-man affair which burst out on the conference floor of the Assembly Hall itself before the conference began. It was the more boisterous of the two. It took several policemen to subdue the Rev. Henry Muir of the Yahwah Little Church, Pembroke Hall, St Andrew, and of the United Progressive Party (UPP), and his assistant, M.A. McLean, who described himself as the first assistant secretary of the UPP.[6]

Thereafter, the proceedings of the conference continued peacefully, and in the end were regarded as highly successful.

Less than one year later, Sangster brought the world to Jamaica again. This time it was the Commonwealth Finance Ministers Conference. This conference held annually in a different Commonwealth country was preliminary to the world financial conference of the International Monetary Fund and World Bank which would take place in Washington D.C. a week later. These talks, officially a conference of the Commonwealth Economic Council, were a recent development in the interchange of ideas between the member nations of the Commonwealth and, together with such Commonwealth conferences as the education talks in Canada the previous year and the medical discussions to begin in London the following week, underscored the new role of the Commonwealth Association on behalf of its member nations.

The *Daily Gleaner* in its editorial on September 22, 1965, noted that the fact that Jamaica was selected for the talks was "a tribute to Mr Sangster's impressive support for the Commonwealth idea. This has earned him high regard in all Commonwealth countries and this regard has been transferred to the Jamaican nation as a whole". The Conference lasted two days, on September 22 and 23. The communiqué issued at the end said:

> The Ministers discussed developments in world economy and expressed concern at the slowing down of the current growth rate of developing countries following a substantial decline in cocoa and some other commodities.
>
> The Ministers agreed that it was desirable to consider at an early date what action could be taken to work out arrangements to provide for more stable and acceptable price levels for commodities that are important to Commonwealth countries. And in this respect, it was agreed to invite the Commonwealth Trade Ministers to consider this problem at their forthcoming conference next year.
>
> In connection with the problem of international liquidity, the ministers were agreed that any new arrangements for the provision of international liquidity should be designed to meet the need of all countries, and the International Monetary Fund should be closely associated with the working out of any new arrangements.[7]

18 | THE KING OF KINGS

In addition to conferences, there were visits by individuals of international prominence. First was Dr Martin Luther King, Jnr, Nobel Peace Prize winner and USA Civil Rights Leader. He came to deliver the valedictory address for graduating students of the University of the West Indies in 1965. Later in the year, the first Canadian prime minister in office to visit Jamaica, the Rt. Hon. Lester B. Pearson, came for discussions with Sangster in his capacity as acting prime minister on matters of common interest to both countries.

Then in March 1966, Her Majesty Queen Elizabeth II, accompanied by her husband, H.R.H. Prince Philip, Duke of Edinburgh, arrived for a four-day visit. While here, she opened the 1966/67 session of the Jamaican Parliament. It was Sangster who handed her the speech she delivered.[1]

But, perhaps Donald Sangster's most acclaimed foreign effort and which elicited the greatest national response was the one inviting His Imperial Majesty Haile Selassie I, Emperor of Ethiopia, to visit Jamaica.[2]

When Haile Selassie I was crowned emperor in Addis Ababa on November 2, 1930, a report of this enthronement was published the following day in The *Daily Gleaner* on the front page. It was a significant event in world history in that it was noted that the Ethiopian monarchy was descended from the line founded by King Solomon and the Queen of Sheba. Indeed, he was the 225th monarch of the Solomonic Dynasty. As such, he was a live descendant of the Biblical House of David.

At that time, Victoria Park in Kingston (now St William Grant Park) was a haven for unemployed or spasmodically employed men who gathered under the giant banyan trees every day. One man purchased a copy of the *Gleaner*, and each took turns to read the news items. Jamaican sailors returning home brought newspapers from abroad to the park and these were also read. Serious discussions took place among these men about the news. The report of the crowning of this Black African Monarch and its possible implications for Jamaica was analyzed for days.

Leonard Howell, a Jamaican, was present in Addis Ababa at the coronation. Another Jamaican, H. Archibald Dunkley, on hearing the debates at Victoria Park, gave up his job as a seaman to, according to him, "study the Bible to find out whether it had any lessons which would identify the emperor as the Messiah of whom Marcus Garvey had reportedly said recently: "Look to Africa when a black King shall be crowned, for the day of deliverance is near"".

Ras Tafari became their king; Rastafarianism their religion.

These two men, along with Henry Dunkley, Nathaniel Hibbert, Altamont Reid, Joseph Hibbert, Vernal Davis, Paul Erlington and Rupert Hinds, were the early pioneers of the Rastafarian movement in Jamaica. They were serious students of the Bible and Marcus Garvey's teachings, and in due course they and their followers adopted Selassie as the Black, reincarnated Christ.

By the 1960s, the movement had grown to thousands. Based on their interpretation of certain scriptures, including Ezekiel 5, many Rastafari wore beards and let their hair grow. Some also began wearing locks, or dreadlocks, which related to the reference to the Nazarite vow in Numbers 6: I, 11, V. Instead of the title, "Mr", they used the word "Ras". Many wore robes and carried staffs and all professed a desire to be returned to their spiritual home which was Ethiopia. Indeed they had seen early maps of Africa which named that entire continent, Ethiopia.

From as far back as 1920, the King and Queen of Abyssinia had sent greetings to Marcus Garvey and delegates attending the 3rd Convention of the Universal Negro Improvement Association held in New York. Their Majesties also invited Garvey and the delegates to return to their homeland where "their race originated and where it can be lifted to its highest place of usefulness and honour, where there is absolute room and great opportunity, and where destiny is working to elevate and enthrone a race that has suffered slavery, poverty, persecution and martyrdom, but whose expanding soul and growing genius is now the hope of many millions of mankind". This invitation became an essential in the Rastafarian creed.[3]

Howell and many Rastafarians rejoiced when they learned that Una Marson, a Jamaican poet who had been living and working in England during World War II, was invited by the Emperor to be a member of his delegation to Geneva, Switzerland.[4] There he addressed the League of Nations to invite the organization to send troops to Ethiopia to drive out the Italian troops who had invaded the country.

In 1937, the Ethiopian World Federation was founded in New York City under the patronage of the Emperor. Its aim was "to effect the unity and solidarity of Black peoples of the world and to defend the sovereignty of Ethiopia". The first Local of the Federation was established in Jamaica in August 1938. In July 1950, the Emperor granted 500 acres of land at Sashemane in Ethiopia for Africans who wanted to repatriate to Africa. The offer made it clear that land would only be provided to skilled persons such as carpenters, painters, plumbers, electricians, upholsterers, and cabinet makers. The offer was made because of the continuous support by the Federation to the Emperor and Ethiopia "through the many trying years of their problems".[5]

Rastafarians also hoped the Emperor would visit Jamaica, so when in 1954 Noel Nethersole, a vice president of the People's National Party made a proposal to the government to invite him to pay an official visit to Jamaica, the West End Ethiopian League bestowed on him the honorary title of Ras.[6] Shortly after, General Quao of the Maroons told a public meeting at the Ward Theatre in

Kingston that his people would invoke their sovereignty and invite Haile Selassie I to visit Jamaica if the government failed to do so.[7]

The Government and Jamaicans had an ambivalent attitude towards Rastafarians. From as far back as 1941, an invasion by the police of Pinnacle, Howell's camp in St Catherine, resulted in many of his followers being sentenced to prison terms with others scattering across the island and into Kingston. From then, police activity against them increased and with the criminalization of marijuana around 1957, Rastafari became obvious targets since marijuana was a core element of their religious practices. And unfortunately for the Rastafarians some of them were influenced into criminal activities because of their interaction with hardened criminals during their prison sentences for marijuana-related offences. In addition, criminals began to wear beards as they found this 'disguise' useful in gaining access to inner-city areas, ganja and information.

The public regarded Rastafarians as either curiosities or madmen. In the meanwhile, children of middle and upper-class families were attracted to the movement and became Rastafarians.

Rastafarians had, by this, become concerned about the misunderstanding by the Government and general population of what and who they were. They therefore approached the University of the West Indies and asked for a study of their history and their beliefs. As a result, a study by Professor M.G. Smith, Roy Augier and Rex Nettleford was done. One of the recommendations of the study was that a mission should be sent from Jamaica to sound out the possibilities of migration to African countries. The study was sent to Premier Norman Manley and he agreed to send an unofficial mission to Africa for this purpose.[8]

This mission was led by Dr L.C. Leslie, a well-known Pan-Africanist. Other members were Rastafarians Mortimer Planno, Douglas Mack, and Filmore Alvaranga, and representatives of various African organizations in Jamaica, Z. Munro Scarlett, Cecil Gordon and W.M. Blackwood. The group spent two months visiting Ethiopia,

Nigeria, Ghana, Liberia and Sierra Leone, and returned home on June 2, 1961 to a rousing welcome by some 3,000 persons, mainly Rastafarians.[9]

Rastafarians continued to venerate Haile Selassie I and in 1961, Clyde Hoyte who was the editor of the newspaper, *Public Opinion*, wrote the personal secretary of the Emperor asking him to say whether or not Selassie considered himself to be God:

> It had been hoped that one of the things which would have been achieved by the recent visit by a delegation of Rastafarians and African-based organizations in Jamaica to Ethiopia was a disposal once and for all of this belief. As a responsible newspaper we desire to do what we can to restore the Rastafarians in our community. To this end, we ask you to assist us by asking His Imperial Majesty to honour us with answers above his signature to the questions listed on the attached page.[10]

These questions basically asked the Emperor to say whether or not he considered himself to be God.

A reply was received by Hoyte from Meba Selassie Alemu, director-general of the Press and Information Department of His Imperial Majesty's private cabinet:

> I have received your letter dated July 27, 1961, together with your questionnaire and the article that appeared in *Public Opinion* in regard to the belief of the Ras Tafarians.
>
> My August Sovereign His Imperial Majesty Haile Selassie I, has read the article with great interest and thereby has ordered me to convey to you and to the Ras Tafarians, His deep appreciation of the warm feeling tendered by the Ras Tafarians towards the Ethiopian people and the Emperor. Nevertheless, my August Sovereign desires to make a citation from the words of the Bible, in which it is said that man should not worship Man, and there is one, and only one God—the creator of the Universe.

Consequently, it is the fervent desire of His Imperial
Majesty that the Ras Tafarians should discard this belief. On
the other hand, my August Sovereign wants the Ras Tafarians
to understand that He is always willing to maintain a friendly,
fatherly and brotherly attitude towards them, and also to be
on their side whenever they need His help.

That did not stop the Rastafarians from believing that the
Emperor was God. It did, however, inspire some Rastafarians
to review and reconsider aspects of their philosophy which had
previously been carved in the bedrock of their beliefs. This change
began in western Kingston. The leader was a 35-year-old carpenter,
Ras Sam Brown. On February 12, 1961, he started holding a series
of conferences, called reasonings by Rastafarians, to discuss the
pros and cons of becoming involved in Jamaican political activities.
At the end of the meeting, Brown told a reporter from the *Daily
Gleaner* that "owing to the fact that the black man is five to one in
Jamaica, it is our intention to use the franchise to win a political
victory and by so doing we will be able to choose our own destiny
including repatriating ourselves".

Action came on October 26, 1961 when Brown announced at
a public meeting at the corner of Spanish Town Road and Chestnut
Lane that he would be contesting the Western Kingston seat
for the Suffering People's Party for membership in the House of
Representatives in the next general elections. "The modern trend," he
said, "demands that the Rastafarian Movement should seek political
recognition, although repatriation to Africa is still a priority for us."[11]

He was one of 112 persons who were nominated on March
19, 1962 for the elections scheduled to take place on April 10, 1962,
becoming the first Rastafarian to contest an election since the
inception of the movement some 30 years before.[12] Dudley Thompson,
who was recently appointed a Queen's Council, was the first to
arrive at the Savage Memorial Hall Nomination Centre. He walked
to the polling station smoking a long cigar and wearing a leopard-

skin belt. Thompson, however, allowed Byron Moore, the People's Political Party's candidate who arrived after him to be nominated first. Brown arrived with a crowd of his supporters. He wore a cap with a photograph of Haile Selassie, and one of his supporters shielded him with a red, yellow and green cloak. The other candidate was Edward Seaga of the Jamaica Labour Party. Thompson was the candidate for the People's National Party. Brown was an independent candidate. He was one of eight independent candidates nominated.[12]

The elections were called by Manley to ask the people to decide the composition of the government which would lead Jamaica into independence on August 6.

Brown's slogan for the campaign was "Black Justice Now or Judgment". He polled 78 votes; Moore received 249, Thompson 5,171 and Seaga 5,851. Overall, the Jamaica Labour Party polled 288,130 votes or 49.63 percent of the total votes polled, while the People's National Party polled 279,771 votes or 48.19 percent of the total number of votes polled. The difference between the parties was therefore slight—a matter of 8,359 votes or less than 1.4 percent. It was described by the *Daily Gleaner* as "the quietest in the island's modern history". For the first time there were no deaths directly attributable to the campaign and incidents of violence were relatively few.

In late 1961, the government had sent another team of Jamaicans which included civil servants, Afro-Jamaican organizations and Rastafarians on a fact-finding tour of Africa to ascertain the possibility of migration by Jamaicans to Ghana, Nigeria and various other countries. The team met with senior government officials in these countries, including Haile Selassie.

This team returned to Jamaica in March 1962. Their report held little hope of a flow of migrants from Jamaica to the African countries which were visited. Indeed, the report pointed out that spokesmen for these countries emphasised their desire to attract only skilled craftsmen and professionally trained personnel such as teachers. And among the Rastafarians there were few, if any, of these persons in these categories. That, of course, did not diminish the belief of Rastafarians that it was their destiny "to return to their homeland in Africa".

The Mission returned to Jamaica one month before the April 1962 general elections when Jamaicans chose the Jamaica Labour Party to lead them into Independence.

Shortly after these elections, a delegation of Rastafarians met with the newly-elected premier, Sir Alexander Bustamante. The meeting was to begin negotiations for free ship facilities for their repatriation to Ethiopia. They informed Bustamante that it was their desire to renounce Jamaica for the Kingdom of Ethiopia and they wished to become Ethiopian nationals under Emperor Haile Selassie I. Shortly after, another group of Rastafarians announced similar intentions.[13]

Now, among his other qualities, Sangster was also an opportunistic politician. He had known of the yearning by the Rastafarians "to return to Africa" and in particular to Ethiopia. He recalled the harsh measures instituted by his government including the arrest of scores of Rastafarians in April 1963 following the murder of two policemen and three civilians in Coral Gardens, St James by six bearded men. The police had claimed these bearded men were Rastafarians, which they, the Rastas, denied, and the Government had not been forgiven for the ruthless harassment of members of the Movement, including forcibly cutting their hair and shaving their beards.

He was also aware of their desire for the Emperor to visit Jamaica. So on learning four years later that Selassie had accepted an invitation from Trinidad & Tobago to visit that country he immediately asked Hugh Shearer, who as a minister without portfolio had the day-to-day responsibility for Jamaica's external affairs, to discuss the possibility of the Ethiopian leader visiting Jamaica during his Caribbean visit with the Ethiopian Mission to the United Nations.

The invitation was accepted. The announcement was generally received with enthusiasm. He was the first African head of state to visit Jamaica since Independence and the first African monarch to do so. His visit therefore had special significance to Jamaicans, and members of the Rastafarian faith in particular.

Sangster was also able to announce that the Emperor had offered a contribution to the government for educational purposes, as a result of which a junior high school would be built in the Delacree Road area off Waltham Park Road in southern St Andrew. The school would be named the Haile Selassie Junior Secondary School. This was a political plus for Sangster and the government.

April 21, 1966, saw the arrival of His Imperial Majesty Haile Selassie I, Emperor of Ethiopia, King of Kings, and Conquering Lion of Judah, to a highly emotional welcome of superlatives at the Palisadoes International Airport. From the previous day and night thousands of Rastafarians traveled from all over Jamaica on foot, in cars, in drays, in carts, in trucks, on bicycles and hired buses, and converged. They came from the Wareika Hills, the "wappen-bappens" of western Kingston, from the hill distances of Accompong, from the lush top country of Moore Town in the John Crow Mountains. They came from Vere and Milk River in Clarendon, from the Johnson Mountains in St Thomas, from little villages and big towns all the way across Jamaica from Negril to Morant Point.

They wore African robes and turbans in a kaleidoscope of colours and brought with them thousands of Ethiopian flags and bunting, palm leaves, firecrackers, thunderballs, drums and the Abeng—the famous bullhorn of the Maroons which had echoed across the hills of Jamaica, and in Africa during the wars of the Ashanti from time immemorial. With them, too, were members of Afro-Jamaican Societies in Jamaica.

They captured the waving gallery overlooking the tarmac. All night there was the blowing of the Abeng and the beating of drums. They chanted songs such as "The Lion of Judah Shall Break

Every Chain". The airport authorities were afraid that the gallery could collapse from the weight of the crowd and barely succeeded in preventing more from climbing the stairs. Those who were excluded from upstairs took over the rest of the airport and the roadway outside.

One month before, Her Majesty the Queen and the Duke of Edinburgh had paid a four-day visit to Jamaica. The royal couple was warmly received. Crowds lined the streets and waved Jamaica flags and the Union Jack.

Her reception was however nowhere close to the response by Jamaicans to the Emperor. All morning there was a slight sprinkle of rain, and there are Rastafarians who still claim that the rain stopped and a dove which became the Ethiopian Airlines plane, flew from the clouds.

The crowd roared and rushed from the terminal building tossing the security aside, and raced across the tarmac to the plane, surrounding it. There were shouts of "Black Man Time Now", and "Hail the Man I" and banners with slogans, such as "Human Rights Now", "Behold the Lamb of God" and "Lay Not Thy Hand on the Lord's Anointed".[14] The enthusiasm overwhelmed authority. The police was surrounded. Only the military were able to keep some semblance of order. The result was that the pre-arranged ceremony went by the way. Dignitaries were not presented, the red carpet was ignored, anthems were not played, and in fact, the emperor was hurried to the governor-generals' car in which he made a triumphal entry into Kingston, creating what was the biggest traffic snarl ever in the city.

During the following two days, he addressed members of both Houses of Parliament, was given a civic reception at the National Stadium, was the guest of honour at a reception hosted by Governor-General Sir Clifford Campbell at King's House at which for the first time Rastafarians were equal as guests to officials on the Protocol List, was conferred with the degree of Doctor of Laws Honoris Causa by the University of the West Indies, paid visits to the College of Arts,

Science and Technology and Jamaica College, laid a wreath at the cenotaph in the George VI Memorial Park in honour of Jamaicans who died in World War II and laid the cornerstone for the Haile Selassie Junior Secondary School in Delacree Pen. He finally left Kingston by rail on a journey of eight hours that took him through scenes of enthusiastic welcome at each crowded railway town, marred only in Spanish Town where the police had to use tear gas to disperse the vast throng.

Sangster traveled in the royal car with the Emperor and Jamaica's governor-general, Sir Clifford Campbell, and introduced the many parish dignitaries who met the train at Denbigh in Clarendon, Williamsfield in Manchester, Green Hill, the 1,700-foot summit of the railway line where Sangster hosted a lunch, Kendal and Maggotty. At each stop there were dance presentations by school children, songs by school and community choirs and other forms of entertainment.

During their discussions, en route, Sangster expressed appreciation that by a recent exchange of notes, formal diplomatic relationships had been established, and he assured the Emperor that a Jamaican Mission would soon be established in Addis Ababa. They also agreed that Ethiopia and Jamaica should seek early cultural and other exchanges such as that of skilled personnel, and that trade could be developed between both countries. Sangster also offered a scholarship to the University of the West Indies to a student from Ethiopia to mark the visit of the Emperor which he was pleased to accept. It was all to Sangster's benefit.

Before leaving Jamaica, the Emperor extended an invitation to Sangster and Campbell to visit Ethiopia in the very near future. Gifts of gold cigarette cases embossed with the emperor's crest were presented to Sangster, the heads of the Army and Police Force, and Ivo DeSouza, the chief of protocol.

Finally, he left from the Montego Bay International Airport for Ethiopia.

Selassie's visit was of great significance, particularly where the development of Rastafari was concerned. Having been ostracised and denounced for years by the Jamaican society, the pomp and ceremony of the Emperor's visit, under the aegis of the Jamaican Government and the society's elites, served to thrust Rastafari into a temporary respectability. Prominent Rastafari elders were showcased in the media with the Emperor and other dignitaries. Some feel that this served to make Rasta more acceptable, and to open the way for the commercialization of Rastafari-influenced music from Jamaica, i.e. reggae music, thus leading to the globalization of Jamaican culture and the Rastafari worldview.

So overwhelming was the response to the visit of the Emperor that independent Senator Wilton Hill presented a motion in the Senate one week later proposing that His Imperial Majesty, Haile Selassie should be proclaimed Sovereign of Jamaica instead of Queen Elizabeth II. According to him, the welcome given to the Emperor by the public clearly showed that "there is far more support for Haile Selassie in Jamaica than our alien Queen".[15]

Many gifts were exchanged during the state visit of Emperor Haile Selassie I. Here, Acting Prime Minister Donald Sangster assists while (left to right) Hugh Shearer, Edward Seaga and Clement Tavares look on.

©The Gleaner Company

19 | JAMAICA WELCOMES MORE

Four months later, Sangster was host to royalty, again, when the Duke of Edinburgh, accompanied by his two elder children, Prince Charles and Princess Anne, officially opened the Eighth British Empire and Commonwealth Games on August 3, 1966 and two weeks later the Commonwealth Paraplegic Games.

In November, President Kenneth Kaunda of Zambia, a friend of Sangster's from previous Commonwealth Heads of Government Conferences, paid an official visit to Jamaica.[1] His country, which was formerly known as Northern Rhodesia, had become independent two years earlier. His newly-independent country bordered Southern Rhodesia where its leader, Ian Smith, had imposed a Unilateral Declaration of Independence from Britain while Harold Wilson, the British prime minister, dilly-dallied with an attitude of permissiveness towards this illegality.

Kaunda came to Jamaica on the first stop of a three-nation Caribbean tour—the others being Trinidad & Tobago and Guyana—to give Sangster and the government a first-hand briefing on what was potentially a dangerous situation, to seek Jamaica's moral support at the United Nations and Commonwealth organizations to push Britain into more affirmative action, and to seek trained and professional personnel such as secretaries to assist in the development of his new nation. He also came to thank Jamaica for the support given to his country by Sangster at a Special Commonwealth Prime Minister's Conference held in Lagos, Nigeria, earlier in the year. Sangster had urged and obtained his colleague prime ministers to examine measures to aid the economy of Zambia which had been adversely affected by the Rhodesian crisis.

Addressing a special session of the Jamaican Legislature, Kaunda stated:

> It is unthinkable and it is beyond the realm of practical possibilities to imagine that the four million Africans in Rhodesia will continue under the subjection of the 200,000 white people who exercise their authority purely on grounds of colour. It is inconceivable that millions in South Africa, with South West Africa, in Mozambique and Angola as well as the so-called Portuguese Guinea will subordinate their interests and destiny in the service of the tiny minorities. The under current of irritation and the anger of the masses will build up to more dangerous proportions and blow to pieces the power exercised over them against their will.

He then appealed:

> Jamaica and all peace-loving countries of the world must help to remove the political dynamite being planted in Northern Rhodesia in the interest of democracy and human rights. Nothing short of force or comprehensive mandatory sanctions under Chapter VII of the United Nations Charter will restore the constitutional rights of African people now suffering under the Ian Smith regime.

At the end of subsequent discussions with the Jamaican Cabinet, Sangster reported that The Zambian President was assured of the reaffirmation of "very strong opposition to the continued existence of the illegal Ian Smith regime, and in addition, that despite the shortage of skills in Jamaica and the great need for doctors, nurses, teachers, stenographers, engineers and so on, Jamaica is prepared to offer help including training facilities, depending on the nature of the assistance required".

The visit and the outcome was another feather in Sangster's international cap.

The year 1966 ended with a vacation visit by Their Serene Highnesses Prince Rainer and Princess Grace of Monaco. While in

Jamaica, they flew from Montego Bay to Kingston, paid a courtesy call on Governor-General Sir Clifford Campbell at King's House, and were the guests of Sangster at a luncheon at his official residence, Vale Royal.[2]

It was a year in which he made new friends for Jamaica, Royalty from several countries, and a president, a prime minister and a Nobel Prize winner. And he did so with aplomb, an ease of grace, and made Jamaica proud.

20 | A NO-TAXATION BUDGET

The Estimates of Expenditure for the financial year 1966/67 were laid by Sangster on the Table of the House of Representatives on March 26, 1966. Calling for an expenditure of £76,120,306, it was more than £6 million greater than the previous year's £69,119,740.[1]

There was a steady increase in the annual estimates ever since the Jamaica Labour Party government took the reins in 1962. The Budget then was £46,078,433. It had therefore increased by £30,041,873 in four years, an annual rise of approximately £7½ million.

Three weeks later, he disclosed the welcome news that it would not be necessary to impose any new taxation to finance this expenditure.[2] This, of course, was only to be expected. The ensuing twelve months would be the last full year of the JLP Government in office. At any time before the end of the year or soon after, general elections would have to be called and electors do not take kindly to being burdened with new taxation.

There was no suggestion in Sangster's Budget Speech that he was presenting a pre-election budget. Instead, he was upbeat about the state of the economy.

Growth rate, he said was up from 6 percent in 1963 to 7.5 percent in 1964; and maintained in 1965 despite diminution of income from the major export crops, sugar and bananas. Per capita income was up from £134 8/—in 1963 to £145 6/—in 1966, despite a population increase of 2.8 percent. For purposes of comparison, he quoted the 1964 per capita figures which were the latest available, for Chile which was £130, Costa Rica £113, Colombia £107, Turkey £85, Haiti £33, Pakistan £28, and Ethiopia £19.

He noted that in agriculture there was a decline in food imports for the first time since 1961, and an upswing in local production of food crops, currently estimated at £20.5 million per annum. "If we never did anything else," he boasted, "we set out to regulate the food supply section of the economy and we achieved it in 1965."

He said that manufacturing had now become the largest single sector of the economy. Twenty-three factories were established in 1965, and 32 will be built in 1966, including such major undertakings as the flour and feed mill, a steel plant, a tyre factory, and the commencement of the £3-million expansion of Alcan's Ewarton alumina plant.

He took pleasure in describing the country's finances as sound, and quoted a recent World Bank report which supported this view:

> Jamaica's favourable growth prospects, the Government's prudent financial management, sound and imaginative development policies, and solid internal financing efforts, lead to the conclusion that Jamaica has a very substantial margin for incurring optional foreign debt at conventional terms.[3]

Proof of this was a £200,000 interest-free loan which he obtained from Canada shortly after to finance the construction of 40 elementary schools, to accommodate between 100 and 200 pupils each. Some of these schools were at Belle Castle in Portland, Ramble, Brainerd, Camberwell, Scot's Hall and Martin in St Mary, Kendal in Hanover, Haddo in Westmoreland, Goodwill in St James, Newcombe Valley, Accompong, Crawford, St Mary's, Lacovia and Mountainside in St Elizabeth, Mt. Olivet in Manchester, Osbourne Store and Alston in Clarendon and The Alps in Trelawny.[4] Canada made similar loans to Jamaica in September 1965 to finance the construction of a bridge and a housing development project.[5]

The previous year he had negotiated a £2 million loan from the World Bank for three major road projects. The loan represented half the cost of the projects which involved large-scale improvement of the arterial highway between Kingston and Montego Bay via Spanish Town, Bog Walk, Mount Diablo and Claremont, to include a four-lane highway between Kingston and Spanish Town.[6]

In addition, he obtained a loan from the World Bank[7] to construct 50 new junior secondary schools with accommodation for 33,000 pupils, an increase in the annual output of trained teachers from 350 per year to 1,000 by 1969, an increase of 890 places at the College of Arts, Science and Technology to add to the previous 840 places, an additional 330 places at the Jamaica School of Agriculture to augment the previous 170 places, the construction of 40 new primary schools and the provision of new houses for teachers in remote towns and villages in rural areas. Some of these junior secondary schools were built in Tivoli Gardens in Kingston, Delacree Pen, Maxfield Park and Pembroke Hall in St Andrew, Port Maria in St Mary, Ocho Rios in St Ann, Albert Town and Wakefield in Trelawny, Maldon in St James, Green Island in Hanover, Grange Hill in Westmoreland, Junction in St Elizabeth, Alston, Lionel Town, Mocho and Thompson Town in Clarendon and Glengoffe in St Catherine.

The first sign of an increased popularity for the Jamaica Labour Party came in June when it won 118 seats to the PNP's 91 in the parish council elections involving 12 parishes. The result was that the JLP took control of seven of the 12 Councils.[8]

21 | OUT OF MANY, ONE PEOPLE

Like Norman Manley and Alexander Bustamante, who were his predecessors as heads of the Jamaican Government, Donald Sangster wanted a world where there was no discrimination against people because of colour. Wherever this issue reared its ugly head, in Jamaica or elsewhere in the world, they were quick in their response to seek to cauterise it.

In August 1963, for example, an American poultry specialist employed by the Jamaica Broilers Group of Companies, Hayne Nalley, referred to the white wife of Byron LaBeach, a Jamaican athlete, as "a white bitch and a nigger lover" at the Jonkoono Lounge of the Sheraton-Kingston Hotel in New Kingston. The following day, he was called to Prime Minister Bustamante's office. Present were Sangster, Roy McNeill, minister of Home Affairs and his permanent secretary, and the commissioner of police. They had already discussed the issue. Bustamante was seated at his desk. All the other chairs in the office were occupied. Nalley had to stand.[1]

"You insulted a lady at the Sheraton Hotel last night," Bustamante charged.

"Yes sir. But..."

"No buts," Bustamante interrupted. His words shot out of his mouth as if they were bullets. "Young man you're an undesirable. The police will escort you to the airport tomorrow and see that you leave my country."

Leaving with Nalley the following day was his fiancée, Evelyn Andrade, a former Miss Jamaica.

For Sangster, the behaviour of Nalley was disgraceful. Jamaica had been enjoying universal adult suffrage since 1944. This meant that every Jamaican 21 years of age and over could vote for the individual political party of their choice. This privilege was not enjoyed by the citizens of Southern Rhodesia (now Zimbabwe). In that country, only persons who owned property could vote. These persons were mainly white, and consequently, the members of its Parliament and the Council of Ministers were also white.

This white rule had been in place since the 1880s despite there being four million black Africans in the country and only 220,000 Whites. Politically, the country was a colony of Britain as was Jamaica before independence in 1962. However, in November 1965, the country's premier, Ian Smith, decided to break away from the authority of Britain by issuing a Unilateral Declaration of Independence. This led to a reinforced white supremacy in the social and economic structure of the society, modeled on the apartheid principles which had been imposed and evolved in their southern neighbour, South Africa.

South Africa had begun the process towards total apartheid by passing the Group Area Act under which urban Blacks, Coloureds, Indian and Whites who were already segregated to a degree, were compelled to live in their own areas as designated by the government. To make it effective, every individual was classified under the Population Registration Act, based on appearance, general acceptance and descent and which divided the population into three broad groups—White, Coloured and Black. The country became divided with over 80 percent of the land being given to the Whites and the remaining less than 20 percent to over six times as many Blacks. In a few years, the Blacks were persuasively and forcibly removed from where they had lived for generations and in due course had to obtain visas to enter their previous homelands.

Apartheid in South Africa, and now in Rhodesia, resulted in the best jobs being reserved for Whites, the places where the Blacks lived becoming slums and a better class of education being enjoyed by the Whites. Other restrictions on black Africans imposed, included where they could eat. And civil servants were instructed not to write black Africans as "Dear Sir" as the "Dear" was too friendly and familiar, and "Sir" elevated their social status. Instead letters to them should begin with the word, "Greetings".

When Smith imposed his declaration of independence, Sangster was acting as prime minister. Immediately he announced a ban on trade with the breakaway colony.

Rhodesia, as it was known since the former Northern Rhodesia became independent in 1964 and renamed Zambia, became the second country in Africa with which Jamaica banned all trade. Long before, as in 1959, the Jamaican Government under the leadership of Norman Manley had banned trade with South Africa because of its racist policy which he had described as revolting to the conscience of decent people throughout the world.[2] The policy embarked on by South Africa prohibited all contact, of any kind, between the white minority and the Black majority of its people.

Jamaica was not yet an independent country. Britain was responsible for its external affairs and so South Africa responded by complaining to the British Government, demanding that Britain should instruct Jamaica to rescind its decision "as the action constituted interference with South Africa's domestic affairs". South Africa's Minister of External Affairs said it could not but regard this matter in a very serious light, particularly in the view of the fact that the West Indies Federation, of which Jamaica was a part, was not yet an independent state and therefore sovereign power still rested with the United Kingdom. However, Britain's high commissioner in South Africa, Sir John Maud, told the minister that "the regulation of trade was exclusively within the competence of the Jamaican Council of Ministers."[3]

And that was the end of that.

Manley had also taken issue with British educational authorities demanding that they avoid using the word "nigger" in the text books for children in schools.[4] Manley and Bustamante had also protested in 1956 when Dorothy Holtz, a daughter of Jamaica's accountant general, Noel Holtz, who went to Canada to marry a teacher at Shawnigan Lake School was asked to leave by the headmaster when he discovered that although she was fair in colour she was not White.[5] Since Jamaica was not yet independent, Manley's and Bustamante's protest had to be sent to England which was responsible for the island's external affairs.

Two months after Ian Smith's rebellion, Sangster led a Jamaican delegation for a two-day Conference of Commonwealth Prime Ministers in Lagos, Nigeria.[6] With him were Senator Hector Wynter, parliamentary secretary, Ministry of External Affairs; Egerton Richardson, Jamaica's permanent representative at the United Nations; James Lloyd, permanent secretary, Office of the Prime Minister; R.F. Dunkley, assistant secretary, Ministry of External Affairs who was also secretary for the delegation, and Senior Superintendent of Police Orville Bernard, security officer. The purpose of the conference was to examine measures to secure a speedy downfall of Smith's illegal regime.

On the way through London to Lagos, Sangster was invited to a meeting with British Prime Minister Harold Wilson who was anxious to secure his support for his policy at the conference.[7] Wilson felt that Jamaica's very unique position as a multi-racial nation enjoying the fullest harmony among all its people, enabled it to put forward representations which were not possible for other Commonwealth countries, especially the African nations who were more emotionally and politically involved. Sangster listened politely to Wilson, but held his council close to his chest.

At the conference, Wilson assured his colleagues that an international ban on oil supplies would bring Smith's regime to its knees "in a matter of weeks rather than months". So, after two days of talks, it was decided that the immediate use of force would not take place, but that the effect of the sanctions against the country would be studied by a committee to be appointed for the purpose. Sangster insisted that this committee would also advise Wilson when the conference should reconvene and, in any case, it would reconvene in July if the rebellion was not ended by then.

A closed session of the conference also agreed that the rebellion must be brought to an end, and all persons detained for political reasons should be released; that political institutions should be constitutional and free from intimidation from any quarter; and that repressive and discriminatory laws should be repealed.

And, with the exception of Malta, the conference also agreed with Britain that a period of direct rule would be required leading to majority rule in Rhodesia. Very important, too, was a decision on a recommendation led by Sangster that measures should be examined to aid the economy of Zambia which had been adversely affected by the Rhodesian situation. This was in keeping with an assurance he had given Zambia's President Kenneth Kaunda when he visited Jamaica.

It also fell on Sangster to give the final address to the conference.[8]

The follow-up meeting of the Commonwealth prime ministers took place in England in September, and not July as was anticipated. By this time, Jamaica had gained an international reputation for its balanced view of questions and concern which came to its attention, and it was the viewpoint of Jamaica which was eagerly anticipated by the presidents and prime ministers.[9]

The conference began with a stern warning by Sangster that the Rhodesian issue was one of priority and with the unanimous and unmistakable determination of the African members of the Commonwealth in full cry, Prime Minister Wilson backed down from an attempt to downplay its importance and agreed that it should take first place on the agenda. It was not only the first topic, but it occupied the conference for nine days of the two-week meeting.

The African leaders wanted British military action immediately. In previous years, Britain had not been reluctant to use its might to crush any semblance of rebellion in its colonies. Many of these leaders at the conference, or their leaders at home, had felt the mighty metal fist of Britain when they had raised their voices for nationalism. They had been imprisoned. Ghana's Kwame Nkrumah, Kenya's Jomo Kenyatta and Zambia's Kenneth Kaunda had spent time behind British prison bars in what was to appear as an apprenticeship and precondition for leadership.

Britain had, by then, learned that wars are rarely won by the aggressors. Those who proclaim victory after such conflicts usually find themselves paying for the recovery of the losers who often become economically triumphant. Worst of all, Ian Smith and his colleagues were not Black and as was described also by British Prime Minister Harold Macmillan, were "kith and kin" to the English who had spawned them.

Sangster had become disillusioned with the ineffectiveness of the sanctions which Britain had imposed. He had learned that the embargo was being broken by way of South Africa and the Portuguese colonies in southern Africa. It was also discovered that two British-registered oil multinationals, Shell and the parastatal British Petroleum Company and the French company, Total, were among the sanctions-busters. Sangster made it clear that although Jamaica was a small country with limited resources, it was prepared to contribute both "men and money to any international force under the *aegis* of the United Nations dispatched to bring about the downfall of the illegal and racially discriminatory Smith regime in Rhodesia".[10]

It was then that Sangster's qualities as a top rank negotiator came into play. He brokered the apparently irreconcilable views of some of the leaders of the Commonwealth on the Rhodesia issue, which more than once threatened to wreck the conference and split the Commonwealth. He also persuaded the British Government to publicly declare that there would be no independence for Rhodesia before majority rule was achieved and, furthermore, secured Britain's commitment to persuade the United Nations to intervene in bringing about an acceptable outcome to the Rhodesian situation.

At first, Britain refused to agree to the imposition by the United Nations of mandatory sanctions against Rhodesia. Finally, however, the British Government said it was prepared to agree to the introduction of a resolution providing for effective and selective economic sanctions against Rhodesia in the Security Council of the United Nations.

The Commonwealth as an institution was saved.

And, according to author Anthony Johnson, "Jamaica had broken a tradition, and moved the former colonial countries into a more equal relationship with Britain. It was then Sangster earned the sobriquet, "Mr Commonwealth".[11]

It was not the last time that Jamaica's intervention saved the Commonwealth from breaking up. A few years later, Hugh Shearer played a similar role at the 1971 Singapore Conference of Commonwealth Prime Ministers.

The British newspapers praised the role of Jamaica and Canada in evolving a conference communiqué which met the unanimous approval of the leaders. Shaping this communiqué on the Jamaican team were Hector Wynter, parliamentary secretary in the Ministry of External Affairs and Hartley Neita, Sangster's press secretary.

22 | CLASHES AND CRISES

Meanwhile, there were many within the Jamaica Labour Party who continued to be jealous of Donald Sangster's quick rise and prominence in the party and the government. Let's face it; he had been elected a member of the House in 1949, yet within one year was elected First Deputy Leader.

So, many were the visits made to Jamaica House, ostensibly as a friendly visit and at the opportune moment the visitor would tell Prime Minister Bustamante of some failing on the part of Sangster.

It was one of Bustamante's weaknesses, if not his strength, that he wanted to know everything about everyone and everything. This was the base for his immediate and instinctive reaction to issues which came before him and became part of his fame as a decisive leader. For example, Sir Neville Ashenheim, a solicitor and company director of over 20 of Jamaica's leading firms and a member of Bustamante's first Cabinet, described him in an interview on CBS (Canadian Broadcasting Service) in August 1962 as "an astute man whose many decisions are based on an uncanny instinct which are usually right on-the-button" for researchers to verify. As a result, his lieutenants were easily cowed into acceptance of his autocracy —which he exercised with gentility and a humour which buttered his anger.

George Eaton in his book, *Alexander Bustamante and Modern Jamaica,* refers to a published anecdote that when he became prime minister in 1962, the practice in Cabinet was for ministers to present written submissions on matters on which they wished to have Cabinet endorsement.

> After Bustamante had heard from the senior Ministers as to
> the implications of a particular proposal, he would announce
> his decision. This practice did not meet with the approval
> of one Minister who suggested that the democratic thing
> to do would be to take a vote. 'Vote?' queried Sir Alexander.
> 'A vote? Very well, we will have a vote. Those in favour say
> aye, those against say no. Eleven ayes and one no—me—the
> no's have it, negatived; next matter.

He also gave short shrift to those who criticised him, his trade union, his party or his government. And those who were members of either of these and who dared to resign were subjected to harsh and strong comments. Rose Leon, for example, resigned as chairman and as a member of his party in 1960 and decided to form her own political party. Her constituency executive, however, suggested that in view of her long association with the Jamaica Labour Party she should try to "patch-up" her differences with Sir Alexander.

"Patch-up?" said Sir Alexander when he heard. "My party is whole. It has no tears, so there's nothing to patch-up!"

Sangster knew Bustamante's strengths and weaknesses. He knew, for example, not to disagree with Bustamante in public, that it was wiser to say nothing. He deliberately kept away from Bustamante's mid-morning "soirees" between 1962 and 1964 when Cabinet members gathered in the prime minister's office for an hour or two of political "chit chat", an occasional discussion of a current official project or programme, and swigs of whisky or champagne from Bustamante's private stock.[1] Noticeably absent from these "get-togethers of political minds" – as Bustamante described them— were Hugh Shearer, Edward Seaga and Donald Sangster. Shearer held his meetings with Bustamante in the early mornings or on Sunday evenings. Seaga and Sangster were too bogged down with work to join these distractions.

With Bustamante semi-retired and confined at Jamaica House, these soirees shifted to the Prime Minister's official residence.

Being as careful and meticulous as he was, Sangster visited Bustamante every Friday night and briefed him thoroughly on the issues which were to come to the Cabinet on the following Monday. He subtly found out what Bustamante's views were, and if he disagreed he painstakingly presented his views and his reasons. Usually, the Chief agreed so that when Sangster's detractors tried to undermine him Bustamante was already aware of the circumstances and could dismiss or ignore them.

For example, when Tacius Golding took it upon himself to summon a meeting of the House of Representatives in 1962 and approve a National Anthem of Jamaica while Bustamante and Sangster were abroad,[2] little did Golding know that Sangster discussed his action with Bustamante before they returned to Jamaica. Bustamante, of course, wanted to be identified with important national issues and institutions; and for a National Anthem for the independent nation he had fought for to be approved in his absence was out of the question.

Now, whenever the prime minister was abroad, the Jamaica Information Service sent him daily news advisories by cable informing him of the main stories which were broadcast on radio and television and published in the newspapers. It was such an advisory which brought the matter to his attention. He was livid. He called Sangster who was in the suite next to his in their hotel.

"Did you know of this?" he asked, handing the advisory to Sangster.

Sangster read it and frowned. "Of course not, Chief."

"Well, you make sure you straighten it out as soon as we get home."

Sangster called Golding on the telephone and ordered him to meet at Vale Royal immediately after his return. And it was there he lashed out at Golding for summoning a meeting of the House without his permission. He then instructed him to have the Clerk of the House place a review of the issue of the anthem on the agenda of the next meeting of the House as a matter of urgency.

Golding felt he was justified in his action. It was the end of June 1962. Independence Day was five weeks away. Copies of the musical score would have to be printed and distributed to schools and churches and other organizations. The orchestra and choirs which would be playing and singing the anthem at the National Stadium when Jamaica's new National Flag was hoisted for the first time would have to rehearse it. A decision could not be postponed any longer or the nation could be embarrassed.

Golding felt hurt that he should have been reprimanded like a child in his former school of which he had been headmaster. He knew that Jamaica House would be filled with party officials that night to welcome Bustamante home. He therefore chose to visit the following day.

The housekeeper led him into the living room. Bustamante was there with Hugh Shearer and two members of staff. As Golding entered, Bustamante stood. He knew the advantage of his six-foot-plus height, and used it to daunt those who were shorter. Golding had to tilt his head upwards.

"How dare you?" Bustamante lashed out. "How dare you choose a National Anthem for Jamaica?" he repeated.

Golding stuttered. "Ch...Ch...Chief..."

"Is anything wrong with your telephone? Has anything been wrong with it? You could have called me, but you didn't because you knew I would not have agreed."

Golding continued stuttering. "Don't interrupt me. You're just the Speaker. I am the Prime Minister. Never...never forget that."

"I'm sorry Chief. It won't happen again."

"Sit down," Bustamante said. "What will you have to drink?

This was how Bustamante ended his tirades with others. Golding left Jamaica House two hours later. It was a good thing he had a driver.

It was the same when Minister of Home Affairs Roy McNeill declared the state of emergency in Western Kingston in 1966. The declaration was a direct result of an upsurge of political gang violence in the area during the preceding three months and which had resulted in six deaths. In addition to the murders, hundreds had been hospitalised or injured.

McNeill was advised by the police and the army that the only way to control this violence was to impose a state of emergency. Bustamante was ill and confined to Jamaica House. Sangster, who had been appointed to act as prime minister was off the island.

McNeill discussed the advice he had received with Bustamante and BITU Leader Hugh Shearer at Jamaica House on Sunday, October 2. Residents of West Kingston woke next morning to find that barbed wire had been placed across the roads leading into the area and no one was able to enter or leave without the permission of the military or the police.

Western Kingston was searched house-by-house, looking for arms of any kind, particularly dynamite and other materials used in the construction of bombs such as those which were exploded in the Queen's Theatre on the preceding Sunday night.[3] Searched, too, were shops, offices, factories and other business places. The mine detection squad of the Jamaica Regiment was among units deployed in the area for the purpose of locating bombs or other ammunition hidden underground or in unlikely places.

By nightfall, some 30 persons were arrested on various charges and about 29 others detained for questioning in connection with the various acts of violence which had taken place during the preceding three months. The police concentrated on searching for suspects who were wanted in connection with the recent murders and whom they believed had been carefully hidden by their criminal or political connections in the area. In addition, raids by the police at the West Kingston constituency offices of the JLP's Seaga at Chocomo Lawn on Wellington Street and the PNP's Dudley Thompson at 23 Regent Street, found homemade bombs, revolvers, dynamite and detonators, machetes, knives, ice picks, ganja and barbed wire bats, and the replica of man cut out of ply board which was used for target practice.[4]

Sangster was neither consulted nor informed about the state of emergency.

His doctors had just identified the first signs of a cerebral problem which needed medical attention. He had flown privately to Montreal for a more detailed check-up by a neuro-specialist. The diagnosis confirmed a dangerous tendency towards high blood pressure. True, there was no immediate danger, but the warning was grim. And the day he returned with this fateful knowledge, the first news that greeted him was of the state of emergency called without his knowledge. Even more annoying was that few politicians abhorred violence more sincerely than he, and the fact that adherents of his own party were among the active combatants was an additional heavy weight of concern.

He called McNeill for a meeting at Vale Royal. There, Sangster reminded him that with all due respect to Bustamante, he now had the constitutional authority and responsibility of being the prime minister. There was nothing wrong with consulting with Bustamante—he was the party leader—but because he was on leave of absence he did not have any executive authority in the affairs of government. He, it was who had the executive authority to approve a state of emergency. Not Bustamante.

Sangster pulled no punches. If it meant that his appointment as acting prime minister was to be terminated by Bustamante when he heard what he said to McNeill, then it was Amen.

Bustamante did hear from McNeill, as was expected. But he never commented on it to Sangster. Incidents such as this, however, were one of the main difficulties Sangster had to endure due to the fact that he had to carry the full responsibility of office within the shadow of the incapacitated Bustamante. He was in the position of the captain of an aircraft who was likely to have the controls wrenched out of his hands at any moment. Yet, he bore this paradoxical situation without complaint.

There was also a major Cabinet clash involving Wilton Hill in which, according to *Spotlight* magazine, "Sangster doggedly, decisively displayed a latent quality—gumption and guts".[5]

Sangster was concerned about the attitude and behaviour of some of the foreign professors and lecturers at the University of the West Indies. This University was founded in 1948 as a college of the University of London and, in its first years, needed these academics as there were then very few Jamaicans eligible for these positions. Sangster felt there were now a growing number of qualified Jamaicans who should be given priority for these appointments. Commonwealth members of the faculty would also not be required to hold work permits, but all others would.

On Monday, March 18, 1965, he asked the Cabinet to decide on the issue. It was agreed that Commonwealth members of the academic staff of the university would not require work permits, but all foreign staff members would. Cabinet decisions are secret, but it was reported that he was backed eight to five on his stand. Immediately, minister without portfolio, Senator Wilton Hill walked out of the meeting. He disagreed with the decision for two reasons. One was that he felt that all Commonwealth citizens or foreign nationals holding or obtaining employment in Jamaica should be required to obtain work permits. Secondly, he could find no reason why any category of employees at the University of the West Indies should be exempt from the provisions of the law.

On reaching his office he sent a letter to the Governor-General resigning as a minister with effect from May 31. He also sent a copy to Bustamante with a note explaining he had taken this step because Acting Prime Minister Donald Sangster had forced on the Cabinet a decision contrary to one taken at a Cabinet meeting earlier under the chairmanship of Sir Alexander. On hearing what he had done, Hill's close friends Edward Seaga and Clement Tavares rushed to King's House in a bid to persuade the Governor-General to take no action on his resignation until they had a chance to talk the matter over with the Senator. However, the Attorney-General advised the Governor-General that under the constitution the resignation took effect immediately it was received by him. They were therefore unsuccessful.

Sangster's future could well have been staked on the Cabinet vote. Had the voting been the other way around, he might have found himself precariously perched on a plunging pedestal. Defeat would have plainly meant the Cabinet had no great confidence, if any, in his leadership. It was a critical moment in his career. At a gathering at Jamaica House that evening, he was criticised by Bustamante on the issue in the presence of others. Sangster waited until everyone present left and confronted Bustamante. "Is it your wish that I resign?" he asked. "If so I will resign tonight."

Sangster later confided to his Press Secretary that Bustamante was silent for a while, then burst into laughter.

"When I resign, you can if you want to," he said.

When asked if he would have resigned, Sangster pointed out that he did not tell Bustamante he was going to resign. He asked him, instead, if he wanted him to resign, which put Bustamante on the defensive instead of on the offensive. Bustamante's response, he said, was exactly what he anticipated.

But suppose he had said yes?

He replied, "Well I would have had to go back to my law practice, take over the running of my property and live the life of a country gentleman. Boring, yes; but productive."

Sangster's next test was at the annual conference of the Jamaica Labour Party on November 25 and 26, 1966. Robert

Lightbourne, whom Sangster had appointed acting deputy prime minister nine months before, announced he would contest the post of first deputy leader of the party, an office Sangster had held uncontested for seventeen years.

It was no surprise to Sangster. He had known of Lightbourne's desire to not only be the first deputy leader of the party but also to be Bustamante's successor whenever the Chief decided to retire. And it was clear that this would be soon. Sangster was disturbed, but not worried, and greater confidence that Lightbourne would not succeed came when Hugh Shearer, Clement Tavares and Edwin Allen decided to campaign for him.

The party conference took place at the Ward Theatre. Hector Wynter was sitting on the platform beside Sangster when Lightbourne arrived for the elections on the first day. Wynter recalled:

> It was a triumphant entry. He entered the hall hoisted on the shoulders of supporters. Before and behind him were two parties of drummers I later learned they were well-known Kumina drummers from St Thomas—and it was like thunder. Delegates on the conference floor leaped from their seats and began dancing to the hypnotic beat.
>
> I turned to Sangster who was watching Lightbourne's entry. His face was expressionless. "The man has plenty support," I said. Sangster gave his characteristic shrug which had become his talisman in diplomacy as well as in difficulty. "We'll see what we will see," he said softly.[6]

It was a resounding defeat for Lightbourne. He received 303 votes to Sangster's 808.[7] He had been elected second deputy leader the previous year and based on his place in the hierarchy, Sangster had appointed him acting deputy prime minister when he felt the need for one. Now, Lightbourne was no longer an officer as these posts were won by Clement Tavares, second deputy leader and Edwin Allen, third deputy leader. Bustamante was, of course, re-elected leader by acclamation.

Sangster did not terminate Lightbourne's appointment as second deputy leader.

Sangster's next clash with a Cabinet colleague was again with Lightbourne. This time it was after the February 1967 general elections which were won by the Jamaica Labour Party. Sangster was appointed prime minister. The day after he was sworn-in he invited all the previous members of the Cabinet to a meeting at Vale Royal where he offered to re-appoint them to the offices they had held before the elections. All agreed. Lightbourne, however, insisted on also being appointed deputy prime minister, the post in which he had been acting. When Sangster told him he would not, he walked out of the meeting.[8]

He did not turn up next day at King's House to be sworn-in as a member of Sangster's Cabinet along with his previous colleagues.[9]

23 | PREPARING TO RING THE BELL AGAIN

It was inevitable, of course, that general elections would be held in 1967, the first such since Jamaica became an independent nation in 1962. Constitutionally these were due by April as this was five years since the last time they were held. The elections could also be postponed until July, a grace period which was also allowed in the nation's constitution.

Both Acting Prime Minister Sangster and Opposition Leader Norman Manley made passing references to the upcoming elections in their 1967 New Year's messages to the nation.[1] Manley's New Year wish for Jamaica was:

> Those who want work may find it, that the hardships of poverty may be eased, that sickness may be healed, that sorrow may find comfort and solace and hope, that the nation may find its way through the difficulties and dangers that lie ahead of us and that we may be restored to a new level of harmony and goodwill and friendship between man and man, and that we may renew our love for Jamaica and our determination to help her to stand on her feet and stride forward as a truly independent country.

In drafting the message for Sangster, his Press Secretary asked him how much emphasis should be placed on the coming elections. "Not much" was the answer. He continued:

> People are now preparing to go to New Year Eve's Watchnight services, New Year's Balls, and home parties. On New Year's Day there will be cricket matches between villages, visiting families and going to the beaches, and they do not want to be overly distracted with politics and elections at this time.

Like Manley's, Sangster's message was brief. "Democracy," he said, "demanded the maintenance of high ideals and a certain level of conduct and I therefore appeal to all to preserve and hold fast to the standards which have given us the stability we now enjoy."

And referring to the elections, he mentioned that it would be a time to decide whether the government of the past five years had done what the people wanted the government to do.

"Prosperity for Jamaica was our purpose when we started and we think we have achieved the goals we promised," he said. "Others may think otherwise. This difference of opinion is a good thing for we are a democratic country in which it is the right of the individual to express his or her own views."

As Sangster had observed, at the New Year, Jamaicans played cricket and congratulated the winners over drinks in village bars, went on outings to Dunn's River Falls and Al Terry Beach in St Ann, or enjoyed a day of racing at the Boston horse racing track in Portland which was attended also by a large number of tourists with music played throughout by the Jamaica Military Band. Others danced all night to rock steady songs which had replaced the ska two years earlier. Hits included "It Comes and Goes" by The Melodians, "You and Your Smiling Face" and "On the Beach" by The Paragons, "Cry Tough" by Alton Ellis and "Take It Easy" by Hopeton Lewis.

Thousands attended watchnight services in churches. Others danced out the Old Year and welcomed the New Year singing "Auld Lang Syne" at night clubs, the ballrooms in hotels and at house parties.[2]

At midnight, lights were dimmed and in the dark there were hugs and kisses and resolutions and promises to love, honour and obey. Ships in the Kingston harbour blew their horns loud and long. There was a fireworks display from the Marina Pier at the Myrtle Bank Hotel. And, despite warnings by the police, there were firecracker explosions all over the island.

Ingrid Chin and the Carnations and Tommy McCook and the Supersonics spurred the feet of dancers at the National Arena. At the Myrtle Bank Hotel tourists and Jamaicans "swung and swayed" to the music of "Los Cabelleros", while at the Sheraton Kingston the Dennis Sindry Band kept the crowd in a lively mood in the ballroom. Lord Jellicoe and his calypso band entertained guests in the Jonkanoo Lounge. Aubrey Adams and Ernest Ranglin were at the Courtleigh Manor Hotel while Ossie DaCosta, the singing pianist, played romantic tunes at the Terra Nova Hotel.

At the St Andrew Club it was Byron Lee and the Dragonaires. At the Flamingo Hotel, pianist Frankie Bonitto featuring balladeer Hugh Faulkner and his band had about 400 guests dancing until the wee hours of the morning. Sonny Bradshaw and his Seven had dancers swinging and swaying at Frenchman's Cove in Portland, while the Jolly Boys' Band played calypso music for dancing at the Blue Lagoon near Port Antonio. The Baby Grand Club in Cross Roads presented a floor show starring Mademoiselle LaChotti, a Jamaican rhumba dancer who had just returned from a European tour and who had the crowd shouting for more and applauding wildly when she gave some acts of torrid Oriental shaking and belly dancing.

Kingston enjoyed visits by five cruise ships with over 2,000 passengers—the *Federico C, Stella Polaris, Regina, Queen Anna Maria* and *Santa Paula*.[3]

Fun and frolic continued on New Year's Day at the Ward Theatre in Kingston where there was a three-hour stage show presented by Ed "Bim" Lewis. Lyn Tait and the Comets provided the music, and artistes featured included Hortense Ellis, Hyacinth Clover, David Isaacs, Angela McKenzie, The Sensations, The Melodians, Pea "Dynamite" Brown, Dawn Penn, Sebastian the Great, Prince George, The Little Twisters, Lloyd and Glen, and rhumba dancers, Senorita Esmarine and Sandra the Fireball.[4]

All in all, it was a happy New Year.

The *Sunday Gleaner's* political reporter selected the minister of home affairs as the "1966 Political Man of the Year".[5] Other potential choices," he wrote, "included Hopeton Caven, Tony Spaulding and Dudley Thompson who he described as "a greatly misunderstood trio who gave the PNP top leaders a certain amount of political indigestion", Edward Seaga and Donald Sangster. He did not choose either of these last two. He thought that Sangster both failed to and did exert a lot of personal influence on Jamaica's politics, but it was difficult to select him as his every act or omission affected Jamaica. And, although he had widened his own personal political picture, it could not be said he had a distinctly individual effect on the island's political life. Nevertheless, he did commend Sangster for single-handedly keeping the Jamaica Labour Party together despite attacks from all sides, while, "Seaga was at the centre of every violent controversy."

Whether Sangster received accolades from the *Gleaner's* political reporter, or not, the fact was that he had earned the respect of the members of the Jamaica Labour Party for his leadership role, and similar approval from the general public. Coupled with this, was a sympathetic feeling for him for having been clothed with the status of acting head of government for such a long time without the mantle of full authority.

Up to the end of the first week of January, the Jamaica Labour Party had not named many of its candidates while by the start of the New Year, the People's National Party had named its candidates for all but two constituencies. One change was made in St Catherine North when Dr Kenneth McNeill, the younger son of former member of the Legislative Council for St Catherine, Eustace McNeill, withdrew his candidacy and was replaced by Ben Cox, a teacher and former member of the House of Representatives.[6]

The next major change in the slate of candidates was the selection of Michael Manley as the PNP candidate for Central Kingston, replacing the party's first vice president, Wills O. Isaacs.[7]

An internal party survey indicated that Isaacs who had been the member of the House of Representatives for Central and East Central Kingston since 1949 had lost the support of voters in the constituency. He was, therefore, named as the party's candidate for North Eastern St Ann, a safe PNP seat. To accommodate him, the sitting member in North Eastern St Ann, Edwin Tucker, stood down at the request of the party executive. The official reason given for Isaacs' switch was that the party wanted its top leadership to be more dispersed throughout the island rather than be concentrated in the corporate area.

It was not only on electioneering that Sangster was working. He gave Jamaicans the good news on January 10, of the formation of a new bank in Jamaica, to be known as the Jamaica Citizens Bank. Most important of all was that the capitalization of £2 million would be owned 51 percent in Jamaica and a minority 49 percent by Citizens and Southern Bank of Georgia, USA. In addition, the majority of the members of the Board of Directors were Jamaican nationals, with A. Russell Graham, Custos of St Andrew, business executive, company director and motion picture distributor as its chairman.[8]

It was Sangster's second announcement connected with banking in three months. Late the previous year he had announced that the Bank of Nova Scotia was localizing its activities in the island.[9] It was also announced that Jamaica's newest alumina operation, the consortium of Reynolds, Kaiser and Anaconda, would increase its annual capacity from 875,000 short tons of alumina to 950,000 short tons and that construction of the plant at Nain in St Elizabeth would begin shortly and start operating in two years.[10]

Sangster also continued to tangibly demonstrate the declared policy of the government of co-operating closely with the countries of Africa at the United Nations, and elsewhere, in the struggle against apartheid and any other form of discrimination. This was made evident when he announced that the government had decided to make a contribution of £350 each to the international funds to assist the victims of apartheid. The funds were the United Nations Trust Fund for South Africa, and the Defence and Aid (International).[11]

Signals began to be sent by the government that general elections were imminent. The first was when Sangster tabled a motion in the House on January 17, "to provide for the issue of warrants by him for the withdrawal of such sums from the Consolidated Fund for carrying on of the public business for a period not exceeding four months".[12] Normally, such a resolution was introduced in March and towards the end of the month and only in cases in which it was expected that the Budget Debate would not be completed before the end of that month—the end of the financial year.[13]

So, the early introduction of the resolution—in January rather than in March—indicated to political observers that the House would shortly be dissolved, and since elections might not take place before the end of March or early in April, it was necessary to empower the government to carry on the administration until such time as a Budget could be drafted and approved. There was also the further indication that elections would take place before a new Budget was introduced into the House of Representatives by this early introduction of the motion. According to the *Gleaner's* parliamentary reporter, the betting in House and political circles was that the House would end its present session in another week, and that only sufficient time would be given to the Senate to complete its business before dissolution of parliament, with elections being held by March 28.

The following day, Sangster made a cryptic reference in the House of Representatives to the imminence of the general elections. Answering a question by Vernon Arnett, the opposition spokesman on finance in respect of the resolution seeking the House's approval for expenditure from the Consolidated Fund pending the passage of the 1967/68 Budget and which was tabled the previous day, Sangster responded with a half-smile:

> As is customary, the Estimates of Expenditure are being prepared, and the actual laying on the table of the House will depend on a decision that has to be taken of certain events during this year.[14]

Members on both sides of the House smiled at the reply which parried an obvious attempt by Arnett to get Sangster to give a clue as to the likely date of the election.

Two days later there was a third hint that elections were "just around the corner".[15] This time it was in the Senate and it began when Senator Howard Cooke of the opposition asked if questions which he had placed on the order paper, and which had not yet been replied to, would be answered before the next general elections. The leader of the House, Senator Hugh Shearer grinned and replied: "I cannot answer the question as framed because I do not know the date of the general elections." Again, when the Attorney General Victor Grant sought the suspension of the Standing Orders so that the Senate could take ten Bills sent up from the House of Representatives, there was more reference to the elections. Opposing the request, Opposition Senator Dudley Thompson felt that the Attorney General should tell the Senate what was the reason for wanting to take all those Bills that day. "We are just as anxious for the Government to complete the work of Parliament so as to prepare for the elections."

Once again Shearer deflected the question by pointing out the Bills were non-controversial and so they were not really being railroaded through the Senate. "It is just that the Senate is behind schedule in its work," he said.

The Senate subsequently adjourned "to a date to be fixed", and members gathered in the lobby teasing each other and offering to speak on their opponents' political platforms to give them much needed support.

By then, the Jamaica Labour Party had chosen all but one of its 53 candidates, the exception being Southern Clarendon where the question was whether Bustamante would seek re-election or whether it would be contested by his heir apparent in the BITU (and probably the JLP, as well) Hugh Shearer. It was noted that Shearer had been caretaker for Sir Alexander in the Clarendon constituency.[16] Then the news broke on Tuesday, January 24, that Bustamante would not stand for re-election and that the Southern Clarendon constituency would be contested instead by Hugh Shearer.[17] The decision meant that the next general elections would bring to an end one of the longest continuous memberships of Jamaica's legislature and Parliament. (The other long-serving members were Leopold Lynch, Florizel Glasspole and Ivan Lloyd). It also meant that all 53 Jamaica Labour Party candidates were selected.

That night, Sangster told the House that he had advised the governor-general to issue a proclamation dissolving Parliament.[18] "The Proclamation will be published in the gazette and will become effective at midnight," he announced. Immediately, Tavares and Seaga rang bells, the bells having been adopted by the Jamaica Labour Party as its symbol, to which demonstration Manley intoned: "Do not ask for whom the bell tolls. It tolls for thee."[19]

Farewells were then said to G.W. Aabuthnott-Gallimore, Felix Toyloy, Edwin Tucker, Iris King, Oswald Douglas, Claude Stuart, William Seivright, R. Oliver Terrier, Andrew Ross and Dr Glendon Logan who were not standing for re-election.

24 | THE BELL RINGS TRIUMPHANTLY

A massive crowd turned up in Half Way Tree, St Andrew the following night to hear the date of the elections.[1] The park was full. So, too, were the roads stretching from the intersection at the clock tower. Buses and cars were diverted. Those traveling down Hope Road were diverted along Winchester Road, across the Half Way Tree Road, along Cargill Avenue, up Maxfield Avenue and then down Hagley Park Road. Buses and cars traveling north on Half Way Tree Road were diverted along Cargill Avenue, and up Maxfield Avenue and Eastwood Park Road and into the Constant Spring Road. Traffic along Hagley Park Road was diverted down Maxfield Avenue across Cargill Avenue, Ruthven Road, Winchester Road and up Hope Road.

Sangster kept the crowd on tenterhooks, waiting as he introduced the party's candidates for Kingston and St Andrew. There was D.C. Tavares, Minister of Housing, South West St Andrew; E.C.L. Parkinson, chairman of the party, Southern St Andrew; David Lindo, a young businessman, East Rural St Andrew; Sam Reid, a contractor and builder, South East St Andrew; Lloyd Williams, a barrister-at-law, North St Andrew; Emile (Bully) Josephs, contractor and builder, West Rural St Andrew; Joyce Hill, school teacher, West Central St Andrew; Stafford Owen, accountant, East Central St Andrew; Edward Seaga, minister of development and welfare, Western Kingston; E.K. Powell, electrical engineer, Central Kingston; and Frederick Johnstone, social worker, East Kingston and Port Royal.

Then he read a message from Bustamante, explaining that his reason for not seeking re-election was because his health was not sufficiently improved for him to continue the rigours of political life to the extent that he would have hoped. Only then did Sangster announce that the elections would be held on February 21. It was also, he said, three days before Bustamante's birthday and that the leadership of the Jamaica Labour Party hoped that every Jamaican appreciating the Prime Minister's work over nearly 30 years would want to give him a birthday present – victory in the elections.

The campaign had started the day before with a full page advertisement featuring a photograph of Bustamante, and headlined with the campaign theme:

"THE JLP HAS DONE MORE FOR YOU
SINCE NINETEEN HUNDRED & SIXTY-TWO" [2]

This was the theme of the advertisements which were published every day. It was observed, however, that neither the photograph of Sangster nor any other leader of the party appeared prominently in the subsequent advertisements. This was debated constantly by the campaign team, every day. The problem was that although Bustamante was stepping down as prime minister after election day, he was still the all-powerful leader of the party and no one could predict what he would do. Sangster was the obvious leader of the campaign but he himself was reluctant to be identified as such until and unless Bustamante endorsed him publicly.

The People's National Party took advantage of this ambivalence. At their political meetings and in their house-to-house "walk-foot" meetings with voters they pointed to the absence of a leader in the JLP's campaign. Norman Manley, they observed, was the undoubted leader of the PNP and he was depicted as such in the party's advertisements, in the newspapers and the commercials on radio. The campaign was having a negative effect on Labourites. They felt lost. Then two weeks before election day, the PNP published an advertisement which said:

WHO DO YOU
WANT
TO LEAD YOUR
COUNTRY?

Without Busta,
No One is Certain
Who Will Be The Boss
Of The JLP.

There's No Doubt About It!
NORMAN MANLEY
is the leader of
the PNP

A Party Divided
Within Itself
Cannot Govern.
WE ARE
UNITED!
Vote to be free
VOTE P.N.P.[3]

It became clear to the JLP campaign team that the party had to be identified with a leader. Bustamante had already announced that he had been forced to come to the decision not to seek re-election "because my health has not sufficiently improved to allow me to continue the rigours of political life to the extent that I should have hoped".[4] Consequently, he could not be seen or even perceived to be leading the campaign. It would have been fodder for the PNP's propaganda machine.

Because Hector Wynter had a good rapport with Bustamante he was asked to visit the Chief, as he was known in party circles, and explain the problem. Wynter, a Rhodes Scholar, already an experienced diplomat, and one of the bright minds in the party, obtained an endorsement of Sangster from Bustamante. The JLP was therefore able to respond to the PNP's advertisement with a telling message in its own advertisement.

BUSTAMANTE SAYS:
"I HAVE CONFIDENCE IN SANGSTER
TO LEAD THE JLP TO VICTORY"[5]

A photograph of Sangster standing beside Bustamante was published in the advertisement. The statement by Bustamante related the hard work he had done for Jamaica, the party and his trade union. Then, after paying tribute to his wife he continued:

> Long years of overwork have affected my health, thus my decision not to offer myself for re-election; but as long as life lasts, my advice and help will always be available to my Union, my Party, and my country. One thing sure, the JLP—unlike others—is not divided on policy because the principles I have stood for are there to guide it. We are going into the election completely united as a Party.
>
> It is being suggested that because I am not running for election, the JLP is divided within itself. I categorically deny this. It is not only misleading and mischievous, but savours of false and shameful propaganda.
>
> I have every confidence in the ability of my loyal and trusted Deputy Donald Sangster to lead the Party successfully into the election with the full support and cooperation of my other able Ministers and lieutenants.

It was the first time Bustamante had been as fulsome in his praise for and expression of confidence in Donald Sangster.

Then came February 21. There were now 53 constituencies instead of the previous 45. Polling was relatively quiet with a few worrying incidents, but none of a serious nature. This was a refreshing change from what had been taking place, especially in the corporate area during the campaign. Violence had erupted at Half Way Tree on the night the date of the elections was announced. It was not, however, attributed in the beginning to party politics. Subsequent reports were that a man rode a motor cycle through the crowd and was accused by someone that he had stolen the cycle. He was being taken by the police to the nearby police station when a section of the crowd set upon the police and a melee started. Bottles and stones were thrown and Edward Seaga sustained a cut on his right forehead. Injured, also, was a policeman. Both were treated at the Nuttall Hospital and released.[6]

Five nights later the Jamaica Labour Party's office on Drummond Street and the People's National Party's office on Regent Street, both in Western Kingston, were bombed.[7] There was another incident of bomb-throwing at the Tivoli Gardens housing settlement.[8] An early morning raid by the police on E.K. Powell's campaign office in Central Kingston resulted in the seizure of revolvers, 200 rounds of ammunition, homemade bombs, dynamite caps, and army bush hats. For four days there was violence in the North Street, Spanish Town Road, Oxford Street, Regent Street and Bread Lane areas of Western Kingston, resulting in nine persons being shot.[9]

Other incidents occurred in Greenwich Town in South West St Andrew in which persons were injured by bottles and stones.[10] Sixteen acres of ratoon canes, just sprouting, at Water Works, a property belonging to Astil Sangster, a cousin of Donald Sangster and the JLP candidate for Central Westmoreland, was destroyed by fire believed to be of political origin.[11]

Norman Manley roamed Jamaica speaking night after night at public meetings. The *Gleaner's* political reporter described his activities as "a wide ranging role. He has not had an inactive day since the beginning of the year. In fact, he is stumping the country; that is his role in the election". Allan Isaacs, a former member of parliament for West Rural St Andrew was in charge, overall, of the PNP's election strategy. The running of the election campaign was his business and he was assisted by a publicity committee, and naturally by all the other top members of the party. For instance, Wills O. Isaacs, a vice president of the party was concentrating his efforts in Middlesex with excursions into the northern half of the county of Surrey. Florizel Glasspole's seat in East Kingston was a safe seat for the PNP and so he was able to range far and wide in the election campaign with the county of Cornwall as his special target.[12]

Like Manley, Sangster was seen and heard everywhere in towns, on the plains and in remote villages in the mountains. The campaign symbol for the Jamaica Labour Party was the bell. It was visible in print—in the advertisements in the newspapers, on T-shirts, buntings, posters and banners—and heard loud and clear at public meetings, in motorcades and on radio and television.

The JLP's publicity and propaganda strategy was directed by Edward Seaga. He transformed his home at 2A Ruthven Road in Half Way Tree, St Andrew, into the campaign headquarters. It was staffed with volunteers who operated round-the-clock, writing copy for advertisements, posters, brochures and handbills, drafting the text for national broadcasts on radio and television, and preparing news releases about the activities of the party for distribution to the newspapers. Motor cycles and vans were also available to carry letters and campaign material to constituency offices island-wide. There was also a printing machine which did in-house printing of campaign material. Playing cards and dominoes were at tables under two large tents on the front lawn. There were also a number of skittle tables. Caterers provided the volunteers with food and drink, all day and all night.[13]

The round-the-clock operation at the campaign headquarters allowed the JLP to respond quickly to news reports and advertisements. For example, the PNP published an advertisement on February 16 that "before 1962, the PNP did this and more for you", and listed 21 projects and programmes. This list included the building of the National Stadium, the Sheraton Kingston Hotel and the Palisadoes and Montego Bay International Airports, the offer of 2,000 free scholarships to secondary schools, and the establishment of the Bank of Jamaica and the Jamaica Broadcasting Corporation (JBC).[14]

The following day, the JLP responded with a list of 42 "new projects from JLP brains in 4 years" (double the PNP's number). This list included negotiating Jamaica Citizens Bank, the first Jamaican bank, establishing a Bureau of Standards to safeguard the quality of products on sale, building a frozen food factory to process ready-cooked Jamaican meals, starting Jamaica's first television service, and constructing the Isaac Barrant Hospital in St Thomas and the National Arena.[15]

Stores on King Street in Kingston announced they would be closing at 12:00 noon on election day to allow their staff to vote.[16] Other business places throughout the island did the same. At the end of the day, a total of 446,815 persons or 82.2 percent of electors cast their votes. Of this the JLP received 224,180 or 50.2 percent and the PNP 217,207 or 48.6 percent. The Jamaica Labour Party polled only 6,973 more votes than the PNP, but won 33 seats, and the PNP won 20. Sangster polled 5,040 votes while George Peryer of the PNP polled only 2,187, a comfortable victory for Sangster. It was interesting to remember that it was because Peryer lost his seat which he had won for the Jamaica Labour Party in 1955 that Sangster was able to return to Parliament in a subsequent by-election. Peryer had been trying to obtain the JLP's support for the new constituency of Northern Clarendon but had been turned down in favour of the mayor of May Pen, G.H. Atkinson, a long-time councillor in the constituency.[17]

For the first time since Jamaica gained universal adult suffrage in 1944, too, Bustamante did not vote in a general election. It was also the first general election since 1944 in which he did not contest a seat.[18]

The new House of Representatives had 14 farmers, eight teachers, six trade unionists, five doctors, four barristers, four solicitors, and one each of the following professions and occupations

—sociologist, company director, contractor, industrialist, businessman, insurance salesman, sugar boiler, minister of religion, electrician, secretary, accountant, and an accountant-politician. Of the 53 members, two of them were women—Esme Grant, listed as a teacher, and Enid Bennett, listed as a secretary. Both were members of the Jamaica Labour Party.

The oldest member of the new House was 72. He was Norman Manley, the Leader of the Opposition. The youngest member was 28, Dr Neville Gallimore who succeeded his father, G.W. Aabuthnott-Gallimore, as the member for South-Western St Ann. In fact, there were two members of the new House under the age of 30.

The average age of the members of the House was just over 50. Two were under 30, 21 were in their 50s, 15 were in their 40s, eight were in their 60s, five were in their 30s and two were in their 70s. The second member in the last group was Matthew Henry, the PNP member for Central Westmoreland. The average age of the PNP members was 54½ years, the oldest being Norman Manley and the youngest Sydney Pagon, 41, member for North East St Elizabeth.

Thirty-one of the 33 members were members of the 1962-67 House. Kenneth Wright, PNP in Eastern Portland was a member before Independence. Thirty-one of the members of the previous House who stood for elections were returned. Three members of the previous House who stood for re-election were defeated – Vernon Arnett, PNP, in Southern St Andrew, Clement Afflick, JLP, in Eastern Portland, and Constantine Swaby, JLP, in Western Westmoreland. No minister-member of the House lost his seat, but one minister, Sir Alexander Bustamante, did not stand. Ministers, formerly members of the Senate, who stood for election, also won their seats. There were now six former Senators in the new House.[19]

It was a jubilant Sangster who visited Bustamante at Jamaica House early the morning after the elections. "I had promised Sir Alexander that I would give him a birthday present and a victory for the Jamaica Labour Party. And I have just been to Jamaica House and carried it to him" he said afterwards in a statement to the press.[20] Bustamante, however, regarded it as otherwise. He told a reporter:

> The people have given me a wonderful birthday present. To all the thousands of people who showed their belief in me and the principles for which I have always stood, I can only say that I thank them from the bottom of my heart. It was a wonderful birthday present.[21]

Sangster was, of course, deflated because of Bustamante's cold response and indifference to the birthday present he had given him. He had known that Bustamante had been pressuring Hugh Shearer to agree to take over the leadership of the party and ultimately the government. Close friends of Shearer with whom he confided his concern had assured him that Shearer had been resisting the pressure. Now that Shearer was an elected member of Parliament and therefore eligible to be prime minister, however, Sangster wondered if Bustamante would renew his persuasion to have his protégée change his mind.

He returned to Vale Royal, his official residence, and called the Financial Secretary and Head of the Civil Service G. Arthur Brown and his Press Secretary for an urgent meeting. The purpose of the meeting was to make arrangements for his swearing-in by the Governor-General as quickly as possible. He asked Brown to liaise with R.C. "Roxie" Roxborough, the Chief Returning Officer to let him know immediately he could certify that the Jamaica Labour Party had won twenty-seven seats, which would be the majority in the new Parliament. Brown should then communicate with the Governor-General to set a time for the swearing-in ceremony. The Press Secretary should take a photographer to the ceremony, but he should not indicate to the photographer what they were going to King's House to do. Sangster was very clear; apart from Brown and his Press Secretary, no one else should know he was to be sworn-in as prime minister.

By noon, Roxborough confirmed and certified that the Jamaica Labour Party had won sufficient seats for the ceremony to take place. The Governor-General agreed to the swearing in ceremony at 4.15 p.m. Sangster arrived at King's House wearing a light-blue top hat and tails of the same colour. He was met in the lobby by the Governor-General's secretary, Neville Smith, and the Governor-General's A.D.C., Captain Bert Chung. Also present were his press secretary and Aston Rhoden, a photographer. The party climbed the stairs to the morning room overlooking the acres of broad lawns studded with majestic trees.

Governor-General Sir Clifford Campbell entered the morning room. He shook hands with Sangster and the small group present. He handed the Instruments of Appointment to Sangster and then invited him to take the Oath of Office. Sangster signed the Instruments of Appointment.

The ceremony lasted ten minutes.

Donald Sangster was now the prime minister of Jamaica.

Bustamante was no longer the prime minister. He had been informed by letter earlier in the day by the Governor-General of the change in his status. And, as prescribed by the Constitution, all other members of the previous Cabinet as well as parliamentary secretaries, also automatically vacated their posts.[22]

25 | THE BATON IS PASSED

Aston Rhoden, the photographer who had accompanied Hartley Neita, Sangster's press secretary to the swearing-in ceremony, left King's House and drove to the office of The *Daily Gleaner*. He was a former chief photographer of the newspaper and he was granted the courtesy of using the photographic darkroom to process the photographs he had taken at King's House. He printed one of the photographs and gave it Ulric Simmonds, the *Gleaner's* political reporter. Sangster's press secretary had, in the meanwhile, called a waiting secretary at the Jamaica Information Service and asked her to issue the news release which he had pre-prepared.

There was a scramble of activity in the *Gleaner's* newsroom. It usually took days before the electoral office could certify election results and so this major and important news was not expected so early, moreso, one day after the elections. In fact, up to that moment the main story was of a letter from Her Majesty the Queen to Bustamante thanking him "for all that you have achieved for Jamaica".

A new main story headline, "SANGSTER SWORN AS PM" was prepared. A special editorial was also written.[1] The editorial offered Sangster 'best wishes' and said:

> Few prime ministers, could ever come to office through such complexities and innovations as Mr Donald Sangster.
>
> The vicissitudes of political defeat, personal and party; years in the wilderness, years in assiduous service without any outward show of impatience to climb the ladder; all these stand behind this quiet man who from being one of the youngest to serve in parish government now becomes the youngest ever political head of government in Jamaica.

Sir Alexander Bustamante is a great leader but—as everyone knows—he is temperamental. Obedience to him which has always been Mr Sangster's dedication is no easy role. Yet between the sometimes tempestuous Busta and the frequently apologetic Donald, there was always a nexus of political and personal affinity which has proved stronger than all the other relationships among the vigorous contentions inside the Jamaica Labour Party.

Whereas ministers of rash and radical mien with lively street corner vigour seemed to be more in harmony with the charismatic leadership of Sir Alexander, the quiet administrative thoroughness of Mr Sangster made him almost indispensable in transforming an emotional labour movement into a workable parliamentary party and government.

The critics will no doubt think of the meek inheriting the earth, but it is not all beatitude: the Latin adage suvvitar in modo, fortiter in re (gentle in method, resolute in action) may perhaps more accurately depict the kind of tough but smooth operator that Jamaica has in its new prime minister.

Mr Sangster made—as did a previous Minister of Finance, Mr Noel Nethersole—a special study of the institutions of finance which are important to a developing country. Indeed, these two men have been complementary in developing Jamaica's settled and respected forms of financial management.

If anything causes some anxiety over Mr Sangster's advancement to the office of prime minister, it is the fear that by that very promotion he may not be able to give the bland, patient, but penetrating attention to our financial affairs which Jamaica has learned to respect him for. He is now composing his new cabinet, and the country looks forward to an array capable of generating thrust in the economic and social advancement of the country.

Best wishes and prayers from all go out to our new prime minister.

Meanwhile, the new Prime Minister and the Governor-General spent 15 minutes in a private discussion in his office. Before leaving King's House, Sangster asked his Press Secretary to follow him to Vale Royal.

Bustamante had sent the prime minister's official motor car—a Cadillac—to Sangster. Sangster sat in lonely splendour on the back seat of the car. His top hat was on the seat beside him. The car stopped at the main gate of King's House at the intersection of Hope, East King's House and Lady Musgrave Roads. A policeman on guard duty at the police post walked to the centre of the intersection, halted traffic and allowed the Prime Minister's car to cross into Lady Musgrave Road. Motorists in the lines of traffic which had paused at the entrance to King's House, or on the way down Lady Musgrave and up Montrose Avenue to Vale Royal, did not know the Cadillac was carrying their new prime minister. It was a strange herald.

The car swung through the gates of Vale Royal and on the palm tree-lined driveway and into the garage.

Sangster walked from the car through the kitchen and dining room to the living room of the house. He greeted the household staff as he passed them. They did not know as yet, that he was now the prime minister. He sat with his Press Secretary and spent about 30 minutes discussing the schedule of appointments which had been set up by Arthur Brown and his permanent secretaries, Barker McFarlane of the prime minister's office and James Lloyd of the Ministry of External Affairs.

The appointments included formalities such as courtesy calls by foreign high commissioners and ambassadors resident in Jamaica, the arrangements for the swearing-in of his new Cabinet and a schedule of meetings with the permanent secretaries and officials of the Ministry of Finance to prepare for the presentation of the budget which he was determined to do as close to April 1 as possible. He also informed him of changes he intended to make in

the Cabinet. These would be announced by him when he made his budget speech, and included the appointment of Hugh Shearer as deputy prime minister, the assignment of the portfolio of finance to Edward Seaga, and adjustments to the portfolios of Labour and National Insurance and Education.

With a parting, "See you tomorrow," Sangster walked slowly and carefully up the stairs of his residence to his bedroom, reading the Instrument of Office he had received from the Governor-General 40 minutes or so ago. No wife, no mother, no father, no sister, no brother to hug with joy and share this time of glory and congratulate him.

The Press Secretary called the household staff together in the dining room and told them of Sangster's appointment. They applauded. He left them wondering who would move with the prime minister to Jamaica House, his new official residence, and whether the new deputy prime minister or minister of finance who would reside at Vale Royal, would retain those who remained on the staff.

Politicians are not the only winners and losers.

26 | JOY IN THE MORNING...BUT

Five days after he was sworn-in as prime minister, Sangster invited his former Cabinet colleagues to a luncheon meeting at Vale Royal. After greeting each warmly, he had drinks with them on the eastern verandah. Present were Clement Tavares, Edward Seaga, Hugh Shearer, Victor Grant, Edwin Allen, Dr Herbert Eldemire, John Gyles, Cleve Lewis, Leopold Lynch, Lynden Newland, Roy McNeill and Robert Lightbourne.

Over lunch he informed them that he wished to appoint them as members of the new Cabinet in the same posts they held previously. It was he said, "a temporary "as-you-were" Cabinet. All accepted with the exception of Lightbourne. He had been appointed by Sangster as acting deputy prime minister in late 1965, and wanted to be now named officially as the deputy. Sangster refused. Lightbourne left the lunch; it was either he was appointed deputy prime minister or he would not accept his re-appointment as Minister of Trade and Industry.[1] Lightbourne had been aiming his sights at the leadership of the government through most of his career as a minister of government and a member of the Jamaica Labour Party.

There were, of course, other claimants for the office which was created because of Bustamante's delegation of paper work in order to enjoy the pleasures of the pomp of the office of prime minister. There was Clem Tavares, who believed that by virtue of his election as second deputy leader of the party at its last annual conference, protocol gave him this entitlement. It was known, too, that Bustamante was urging that Shearer should be appointed deputy prime minister since he, Bustamante, had been unable to persuade Shearer to take on the role of prime minister.

Donald Sangster being greeted in England as he deplanes with an entourage including Hugh Shearer, Hector Bernard and Hartley Neita.

A prepared and self-assured Donald Sangster, enters Gordon House, on his way to address Parliment in 1964.

February 23, 1967, ascending the stairs at King's House for his Investiture as prime minister of Jamaica, escorted by Governor General's Secretary Neville Smith (left) *and* Aide-de-Camp *Osbert Chung.*

Bustamante and Sangster lead the JLP Members to Gordon House for the opening of Parliament.

Photographs ©The Gleaner Company

That afternoon, 11 ministers were sworn-in by the governor-general. Lightbourne did not attend the ceremony, but that night, he informed Sangster that he was available for office. Next day, Lightbourne took the oath of office at King's House.

Sangster did not attend Lightbourne's swearing-in ceremony. He had already planned a four-day all island "thank you" motorcade with the other candidates, winners and losers of the JLP who stood for the election the previous week. The motorcade left from the Harbour View roundabout in east St Andrew[2] on the morning before Lightbourne's swearing-in.

It did not have an auspicious start. Harbour View was over 90 percent PNP and scores of the residents turned up at the site with horns and drums, and booed them on their way.[3] After that, however, it was cheers and bell-ringing all the way through St Thomas, Portland, St Mary, upper St Andrew and returning to Kingston that night. The following day the tour started on the Washington Boulevard, went west to Gregory Park, Spanish Town and Old Harbour in St Catherine, into Clarendon including Sangster's constituency, then to Spaldings, Christiana and Mandeville. The third day, the motorcade left from Mandeville to St Elizabeth, stopping at Munro College, where Sangster, Gyles, Eldemire and McNeill reminisced on their school days with headmaster Richard Roper, and to Hampton Girls School where headmistress, Miss Gloria Wesley-Gammon who had known Sangster for a long time gave him a special warm and friendly greeting. From St Elizabeth the motorcade went through Westmoreland, Hanover and ended at Montego Bay. The final day saw the team traveling through St James, Trelawny, St Ann, St Catherine and St Andrew, ending in Half Way Tree where Sangster had announced election day four weeks earlier.

Unlike other stops where he spoke, even briefly to the crowds, Sangster was noticeably tired and drawn and did not make an expected "after-tour" address.[4]

Not known, except by a very few close friends and associates, was that he was a long-standing hypertensive and until then it was largely untreated or undertreated. In 1966 he developed acute diplopia and his physician, Dr A.I. McFarlane consulted Professor Eric Cruickshank and Dr Ronald Irvine of the University of the West Indies. They found him to be hypertensive (195/120) with marked hypertensive retinopathy and a left 6th nerve palsy. Sangster flew to Montreal and was admitted to the Montreal Neurological Institute and Hospital under the care of Dr Francis McNaughton.[5]

Sangster's hypertension was investigated and treated. No neurological studies were performed. It was concluded that he had a "vascular/hypertensive" 6th nerve palsy; and this appeared to have recovered well.

Despite a very hectic programme of speaking engagements and tours of constituencies during the election campaign, Sangster was determined to travel the island with the "thank you" motorcade.

It was a well-established practice of the Jamaica Labour Party to return thanks to the people after general elections—win or lose. The practice has been faithfully followed over the years by the JLP as an act of courtesy by a party which has a regard for courtesy to the common people.

The fact is that Jamaica voted for us and is a simple gesture of courtesy to tell them thanks in person. In addition we wished to let those who did not vote for us to know that we bear malice to none and that our concern is to work for all the people of Jamaica.[6]

Sangster was, however, in a hurry to form the structure of his government and to begin his own administration. To come was the naming of his Senators, the appointment of two of that number to be ministers without portfolio, the appointment of parliamentary secretaries and a leader of the House, the official opening of parliament, finalizing the budget, and then the Budget Debate.

He had received an invitation from the Prime Minister Lester Pearson of Canada, inviting him to visit Canada between August 1 and 6 to participate in the celebrations of that country's 100th anniversary of its Confederation.[7] This would be an appropriate time for him to use that opportunity to attend the Montreal Neurological Institute and Hospital for further examination of his condition. Physically, he felt well; his early training and activities as an athlete, footballer, cricketer and boxer, had stood him in good stead so far. Like all men, he hated the thought of having to see his doctors.

Step by step, the process of forming the structure of the new government began to take place. Despite accusing the government of disenfranchising thousands of voters and mishandling the administration of the recent general elections, the opposition People's National Party recommended the eight persons for appointment as senators to the governor-general as required by the constitution.[8] Two of them were members of the previous Senate— Vivian Blake and Dr Kenneth McNeill. The six new members were Ken Hill, two candidates who failed to win seats in the General Elections—Holroyd Thompson, a trade unionist who ran in Western St Mary, and Maurice Tenn, a barrister, who ran in Eastern St Catherine. The other three were Isaac J. Matalon, a planter and businessman, Carol Reckord, a radio commentator on agricultural topics, and Mrs Venetia McDonald, a primary school teacher in Westmoreland.

Five days later, on March 8, Sangster released the names of the men and a woman, Elsie Bailey, a pharmacist, he was advising the governor-general to appoint as the government members of the Senate.[9] The men were Sir Neville Ashenheim, a company director and currently Jamaica's ambassador to Washington; Cyril Atkinson, agriculturist; Dr Arthur Burt, senior assistant registrar of the University of the West Indies; Rupert Chin See, manufacturer and president of the Chinese Benevolent Society; Allan Douglas, solicitor and former minister of Trade and Industry; Dr Ronald

Irvine, lecturer in Medicine at the University Hospital and a former member of the senate; Gerald Mair, economist and deputy president of the former senate; Joseph McPherson, trade unionist and a member of the previous senate; Ivan Moore, businessman; G.S. Ranglin, teacher and former minister without portfolio; Austin Taylor, farmer and a member of the former Senate; and Hector Wynter formerly high commissioner for Jamaica to Trinidad & Tobago, and former parliamentary secretary in the Ministry of External Affairs.

Removed from membership of the Senate by Sangster were Dr Frederick Duhaney, the immediate past president of the senate; Egerton Wright; and Wilton Hill, a former minister without portfolio who had resigned as a minister over Sangster's decision to exempt Commonwealth citizens on the academic staff of the University of the West Indies from the provisions of the Work Permits Law, who had remained as a member of the previous senate.

Three other former members of the senate, Hugh Shearer, now Minister of External Affairs, Victor Grant, Minister of Legal Affairs and Attorney General, and Esme Grant had won seats in the elections and were now in the House of Representatives.

Sangster completed his Cabinet on March 13 when he named Sir Neville Ashenheim, Allan Douglas and Hector Wynter from the senate as ministers. They were sworn in at King's House the following day. Also sworn in as parliamentary secretaries, were Cyril Atkinson, Dr Arthur Burt and Ivan Moore.[10]

The stage was now set for the first session of the new Parliament. This was, traditionally, a day when supporters of the Jamaica Labour Party gathered to the north of Gordon House and supporters of the People's National Party gathered at the south and cheered their representatives as they marched on Duke Street to the parliament. Tradition was that the Senate met first, the president and deputy president were elected, and then with the clerk of the legislature officiating, all members took the Oath of

Allegiance. The senate was then adjourned followed by a meeting of the House of Representatives. They, too, elected a speaker and a deputy speaker. As with the senate, the members were then sworn-in by the clerk. Normally, there was good-natured bantering between both sides.

Because of his love for Parliament and its traditions, Sangster had looked forward to this day. There were rumours that the opposition People's National Party planned a demonstration, but he hoped it was not true.

But it was not to be.

The morning of March 15 came and Jamaica Labour Party supporters gathered on Duke Street, but except for a few curious people to the south of parliament, the usual crowd of PNP supporters was absent.[11]

In addition, the PNP members of the opposition in Parliament stayed away from the ceremony.

This, however, did not prevent the ceremonials. The senate met and Senator George Ranglin was elected president and Gerald Mair, deputy president of the Senate. Then, with Clerk of the Legislature, Doston Carberry officiating, senators took the Oath of Allegiance, and adjourned.

The House of Representatives then met. E.C.L. Parkinson was elected speaker and Cleveland Stanhope elected deputy. Sangster was sworn-in followed by the ministers. Floor members were then sworn-in with vociferous parliamentary cheers for the two women members, Enid Bennett and Esme Grant.

Robert Lightbourne was the only member not present. Later a message was received from him that he was ill and confined to bed on the advice of his doctor for a few days.[12]

The next item on Sangster's agenda was the budget. He wanted to present it to the House not later than April 1. During the past three months, officials of the Ministry of Finance had been receiving preliminary estimates from the other ministries and had been in discussions with the permanent secretaries. Discussions had also taken place with the ministers, at which Sangster was always present. The stage had now been reached where the budget could be put together in a draft for the new Cabinet to study.

Sangster decided to spend the two days after the opening of parliament, Thursday and Friday, on a retreat in Newcastle at the military bungalow, Bush Cottage, to work on the 1967/68 Budget.[13] Officials of the ministry traveled to the cottage in which he stayed on both days. Together they began to pull together all the financial analyses done by the economists of the Ministry of Finance, the Bank of Jamaica and the Accountant General, summarize them and shape his budget presentation. They worked far into the nights.

He planned to return to Kingston on Saturday morning.

Newcastle is a mountain outpost for the Jamaica Defence Force. Situated 19 winding, uphill miles from Kingston and 4,000 feet above sea level, Newcastle enjoys a year round cool climate with temperatures ranging from 23 to 33 degrees centigrade. It was established in 1841 for the British troops who were then stationed in Jamaica, as it was found that these soldiers were subject to diseases such as malaria and yellow fever. The advice was that people who lived in the mountains did not suffer from these fevers.

At first, the troops stationed at Newcastle lived in tents, but over the years quarters were built for them. In addition, there were cottages for the officers. With Independence, it is part of the Jamaica Defence Force establishment and new recruits do part of their training there. The officers of the Jamaica Defence Force preferred to live either at Up Park Camp or in houses in the vicinity. The cottages at Newcastle, therefore, became available for rental, mainly to public officers and their families. They were fully furnished, with a kitchen and crockery and a stove. Persons who rented them had to carry only food, bed linen and towels.

Sangster was shaving early on Saturday morning when he got the first cerebral seizure. The maid found him on the floor and called a sergeant for help. He was taken to his official residence, Vale Royal. He complained about an upset stomach.[14] A medical team consisting of Dr A.L. McFarlane began to examine him. The examination showed him to be somnolent with neck stiffness and bilateral 6th nerve palsies. A diagnosis of subarachnoid hemorrhage (SAH) was made. This was confirmed by a lumbar puncture which showed "uniformly bloody fluid under high pressure".

The doctors ordered him to remain in bed, recognising the need for him to relax following the recent strenuous election campaign, followed by the hectic "thank-you" all-island tour.

Monday, he was unable to attend what was to be the first full meeting of his Cabinet. However, he indicated that the minister of housing who was the second deputy leader of the party should preside. During the day, further complications developed, among them excessively high blood pressure. The doctors attending him decided that he should be transferred to Canada immediately, to the Montreal Neurological Institute and Royal Victoria Hospital where he had previously been examined and where facilities existed which were not available in Jamaica.

It was Dr McFarlane, the Custos of Kingston and Sangster's personal physician who recommended the medical centre in Montreal. He had spent a short attachment at the Institute and had referred other patients there since then. He, therefore, knew of its work and stature. He had also referred Sangster there before. This was in February 1965. Sangster had then been examined at the University Hospital in Mona by Professor Eric Cruickshank and Dr Ronald Irvine, and also by Dr D.W. Degazon, consultant ophthalmologist, when he complained of diplopia (double vision). This occurred when he looked to the left. Dr Degazon suggested it could be due to a lesion in the left mid-brain and in consulting with Dr McFarlane it was decided that Sangster should go to Montreal for a thorough investigation.

Dr McFarlane fully briefed by Dr McNaughton by letter of February 1, 1966 on Sangster's medical history and requested him to "carry out an investigation". He had also suffered from tension headaches with associated variable high blood pressure for at least 15 years. Earlier in his life —in 1929—he had contracted typhoid fever which had led at the time to some weakness in his heart. He had also had an appendectomy in 1948.

The report by Dr McNaughton and the investigating team at the Institute was signed by Dr R.F. Nelson. It said.

"We cannot feel satisfied with blood pressure readings of 192/130 lying and 168/132 standing. It was discovered that the patient had ceased taking his Ismalin (blood pressure) tablets for over one week. After resuming his medication, his blood pressure returned to 168/110 within 24 hours."[15]

At the end of the investigation and treatment period, he was released to return to Jamaica "to the care of his physicians".

On this second occasion when it was decided to send Sangster to the Montreal Neurological Institute again, there was a flurry of diplomatic activity. Canadian High Commissioner to Jamaica, R. Harry Jay, and Jamaica's High Commissioner to Canada, Vincent McFarlane, jointly made the arrangements for him to be admitted to the Hospital, while the United States Ambassador to Jamaica, W. Thomas Beale, arranged a special jet flight provided by the American Government to take him to Montreal.

27 | SORROW IN THE NIGHT

Before leaving, Sangster named Tavares to act as prime minister, minister of external affairs and minister of defence, and Edward Seaga to act as minister of finance.

The plane left just before midnight on Monday, March 21, and arrived in Montreal the following morning. With Sangster were Drs Herbert Eldemire, Ronald Irvine and John Sandison of the University of the West Indies' Department of Medicine, a nurse, Angelita Leiba, and his political aide and friend, Andrew Abrahams. At the hospital, he was admitted under the care of Dr Francis McNaughton. Neurosurgical consultations were provided by Drs Theodore Rasmussen and Francis Leblanc. On admission, he was drowsy but oriented and had a very stiff neck. The hypertensive retinopathy and bilateral 6th nerve lesions were confirmed. No focal neurological deficits were found; he was therefore a grade 2 SAH (2).[1]

By the next day, Sangster's condition improved. He was comfortable, his usual cheerful self and his appetite had returned. It was then decided that Drs Irvine and Sandison and Nurse Leiba did not need to stay in Montreal and they returned to Jamaica. Eldemire was, however, instructed by Tavares to remain in Montreal to act as a medical liaison between the specialists of the hospital and the Cabinet. Sangster's Press Secretary, who was now performing these services for Tavares, and Audrey Chong, an officer of the Jamaica Information Service, sat in on the telephone conversations from Eldemire and in consultation with Seaga, the Minister responsible for Government Information, provided the news media with regular reports of the Prime Minister's condition during the following weeks.

That same day Sangster had a carotid angiogram which showed slow arterial flow, irregular narrow and beaded vessels, but no aneurysm or vascular malformation. These findings were interpreted by Dr D.I. McCrae, neuroradiologist, as atherosclerotic vessel changes, although in retrospect they were clearly due to vasospasm. The angiogram was performed under general anesthesia, and Sangster had an episode of hypotension during this, compounding the poor cerebral circulation caused by the vasospasm.

In the meanwhile, Tavares was sworn-in as acting prime minister by Governor-General Sir Clifford Campbell at King's House.[2] When he returned to office he received a telegram from Opposition Leader Norman Manley. It read: "Extremely sorry of Prime Minister's illness and hope he has successful and speedy recovery." Similar messages were to flood the Office of the Prime Minister in the ensuing days.

RJR contacted Ewart Walters, a former reporter on the staff of the *Daily Gleaner* who was studying at Carleton University in Ottawa, and assigned him to go to Montreal and provide the station with regular news reports.[3] Hector Bernard, the director of news for the Jamaica Broadcasting Corporation also went to Montreal to file news reports to the Corporation's radio and television services.

It was a tense and sad time.

On Thursday, March 23, a special meeting of the Cabinet was held at which a decision was taken for Minister of External Affairs Hugh Shearer to join Eldemire in Montreal and to liaise with officials of the Canadian, USA, British and other governments resident in Montreal and Ottawa. Shearer had carried out similar functions when Bustamante had been operated on at the Walter Reed Hospital in Washington D.C. two years earlier. The Cabinet also invited Sangster's aunt, Iris Sangster, and her son Dr Alfred Sangster, lecturer in Chemistry at the University of the West Indies, to accompany Shearer. Sangster's aunt, Iris, was one of his favourite relatives and he had asked her to join him as his hostess at many official functions while he was deputy prime minister and acting prime minister. Later, they were joined in Montreal by Sangster's niece, Mrs Donald Kennedy. Tavares also decided that "in view of the state of health of the prime minister, I feel I should be there at this time".[4] His stay in Canada was short and he returned to Jamaica after consulting with the doctors.

Sangster became stuporose (grade 4 ASAH). An intracranial monitor showed raised intracranial pressure which was considered a likely brain endema secondary to ischemia resulting from vasospasm. A ventriculogram was performed and this showed no specific abnormalities. However, he began to get worse. He had a tracheo, a ventricular drain inserted. His hypertension was treated aggressively.

The *Gleaner* reported on April 1 that there was no change in the critical condition of the Prime Minister. The report said he had been semi-conscious in the hospital for almost two weeks and added that the Canadian specialists were keeping him on drugs to prevent blood from a burst vessel in his head forming a fatal clot on his brain.

The report continued with more details:

> Health Minister Dr Herbert Eldemire who has remained at the Prime Minister's bedside during the past two weeks said wearily tonight (March 31) there was nothing he could add about Mr Sangster's condition beyond that it was unchanged but still serious. The minister, showing signs of strain, declined to discuss the clinical details of the case. But other medical sources in Montreal have revealed for the first time just how extremely serious the ailment is.
>
> There are two basic types of neurological cranial haemorrhage: the less serious of the two is when bleeding occurs from a burst blood vessel between the brain and the skull. This condition although serious can be corrected by

a surgical operation and the patient stands a good chance of full recovery.

The other type is when bleeding occurs within the brain itself. Rarely is it possible to operate on such a condition. The medical source in Montreal added that "often a person suffering an intra-cranial haemorrhage within the brain itself, never even comes out of the coma or semi-conscious condition. At the same time they can remain in that condition for weeks or months. It is almost impossible to say how long the condition will continue'.

Obviously, Mr Sangster is suffering from the latter and more serious condition and the specialists attending him have made no attempt to operate. In recent years it was also pointed out he has suffered from high blood pressure and a year ago was examined by specialists at the Montreal Neurological Institute.

The following day Eldemire reported that "Mr Sangster's neurological status and level of consciousness have deteriorated considerably over the past 24 hours. The doctors feel that his chances of survival are becoming progressively less due to the fact that the condition has worsened".

Thereafter, he continued to worsen gradually. No further neurological investigations were performed.

On Thursday April 4, Sangster's Press Secretary issued a one-sentence news release. It read: "There has been some further deterioration in the condition of the prime minister, and the possibility of his survival is now even less".

Two days later it was learnt that although two nurses were constantly at his bedside, and the three specialists were seeing him twice daily, "at this point their examinations are unhappily no more than a statistical recording of the heart beat which is fading now, and respiration which is weakening".[5]

And a report out of Canada referred to "the struggle and

drama that has been staged during the past two weeks: constant injections of the most modern drugs available, the frantic consultations with other specialists and the hopes of the doctors that soared when ten days ago they finally arrested the bleeding from the burst blood vessels in his brain".[6]

From then on, it was only a question of time.

Life, of course, continued in Jamaica. The Eddy Thomas Dance Workshop presented its first full-length programme at the Little Theatre on Saturday, April 1. The nine-year old group presented "Welcome Dance" from "Plantation Revelry", "Bandana Dance", and "Footnotes in Jazz", "Country Wedding" and "Games of Arms". The dances were choreographed by Thomas and Rex Nettleford.[7]

Jamaica drew a Shell Shield cricket match with Guyana at Bridgetown, Barbados. Batting first, Guyana scored 430, to which Jamaica replied with 538, with Renford Pinnock scoring 153 and Easton McMorris 218. In their second innings, Guyana made 399 for three declared and Jamaica barely managed to save defeat when they lost six wickets for 69 runs at close of play.[8]

Locally, Boys' Town's 18-year-old spinner Egbert Gordon took a career best of eight wickets from 44 runs, bowling out Jamaica Telephone Company for 174 in a Junior Cup match.[9]

And the seasonal preoccupation with hats was reflected in the trend of entertainment featured at an Easter Tea Party held by the St Andrew Old Girls' Association in the school hall on Cecelio Avenue in Half Way Tree. A gay cluster of burnt-orange silk petals worn by Joyce Phillips was awarded the prize as the prettiest and "Most Eastery".[10]

Then there were the crazy hats, and the prize went to "Stenographer's Nightmare", an office scene complete with desk, secretary's chair, filing cabinet and the many accessories of a secretary's life, from stencil boxes to paper clips, worn by Joyce Samuel. Second prize went to "Wash Day", a recreation of a laundry scene, from wash tub to clothes line, worn by Carmen Wellington. The third prize went to "Tea Party", worn by Marva Saunders, which showed tea crockery, and pastry and other requirements.

Anticipating that Sangster could die and the Office of Prime Minister could become vacant, Tavares and Lightbourne began lobbying their colleagues in the House for their support. Lightbourne also decided to persuade Governor-General Sir Clifford Campbell, calling on him and reminding him that he had been acting as deputy prime minister for over one year and so should be the logical successor if the post became vacant. He also sent Campbell the names of the persons he would wish to be the members of his Cabinet. Among the names were Emile Josephs, David Lindo and Adrian Bonner.[11]

Campbell, however, consulted with Bustamante in his capacity as Leader of the Jamaica Labour Party. Not only did Bustamante verbally recommend that Hugh Shearer should be appointed prime minister, but he subsequently confirmed it in writing.[12] He was also advised by Attorney General Victor Grant and Chief Justice Sir Rowland Phillips, that in appointing a prime minister he was obliged to choose an elected member of the House of Representatives who was "best able to command the confidence of a majority of members of the House". As such, he should, therefore, seek to find out from these members who they wished to be their prime minister.[13]

On receiving this advice, the Governor-General invited the JLP members of the House to meet with him at King's House. At this meeting he discussed the issue and asked them to convene a caucus and then advise him of their choice.[14]

A sobbing Hugh Shearer and Herbert Eldemire returned to Jamaica on the night of Wednesday, April 5, to take part in what turned out to be a dramatic "cliffhanger" balloting among these MPs for the succession to the post of prime minister.[15]

There were three candidates. Tavares and Lightbourne,

were already named. The third was Shearer who was only recently nominated by Dudley McKenley, a Clarendon member of the House, on behalf of Bustamante.

Just before the voting began, Speaker of the House, E.C.L. Parkinson received a letter from Bustamante strongly recommending Shearer to be chosen. He asked that the letter should be read to the gathering. Parkinson called the three candidates to a private meeting and after reading it to them, suggested that it should not be read to the others as was requested by Bustamante. His reason, as he subsequently explained to Hector Wynter, who was his stepson, was that it had been agreed by everyone that none of the candidates should address the meeting. The letter could be construed as a speech on Shearer's behalf. This would have opened the meeting to speeches by all the candidates and their supporters. It could become long, drawn out, and bitter and it would not have been a good way for the new prime minister to begin his term of office, in a rancorous atmosphere. Shearer was, of course, at a disadvantage. He had been off the island while his two colleagues were campaigning for the office. What campaigning organised for him was done unbidden by Edwin Allen, Dudley McKinley and Victor Grant.

Nevertheless, he agreed.[16]

There were 31 persons present at the meeting. The other two eligible voters, Sangster and Elliston Wakeland[17] were in hospitals. In the first balloting, Lightbourne received eight votes, Shearer ten, and Tavares twelve. One vote was spoilt. It was always believed that it was Shearer's.

Because neither Shearer nor Tavares had obtained a majority, a second ballot was cast. This time, the votes were 15 for Tavares and 16 for Shearer. Shearer's vote was increased to 17 the following morning when on Tavares' insistence, Wakeland was visited at the University Hospital by a small group and his vote was taken by Parkinson.

Tavares and his supporters were not pleased. He had been elected second deputy leader of the JLP after Bustamante and Shearer at the last party conference. He felt that the vote by the members of the House did not reflect the decision of the party's delegates. He, therefore, wanted to take the issue to the Central Party Executive.

He was persuaded not to do so, but the editor of The *Gleaner* learned about the dispute and set the record straight in an editorial:

> It might appear surprising to some that the number two choice of the Jamaica Labour Party Conference was not chosen to succeed Mr Sangster. However, a party conference, in the structure of the Constitution and Democracy should not seek to arrogate to itself the right to choose the leadership in Parliament of members duly elected to that Parliament. The members of a Party are admittedly a special and devoted group of citizens, but they are not the nation. It is the elected members of parliament who are the true representatives of the nation. It is they who have the right, the duty and the responsibility to decide who shall be the accepted leader who will enjoy the confidence of the majority of their number.[18]

During the process of the election, financial secretary, G. Arthur Brown, made reference to it at a luncheon at the Terra Nova Hotel in honour of members of the Institute of Canadian Advertising who were visiting the island. In speaking about the grave illness of the Prime Minister he noted it was a circumstance that everyone regretted and the country regarded it with great distress.

> But the business of the country has to go on, and it is comforting to know that we have been so schooled in the democratic and constitutional process that consultations are now taking place which will, we hope, result in the choice of a Prime Minister who will be universally acceptable to Jamaica. It is good to know that our Prime Minister is chosen, and

let us all see that this is how our Prime Minister will only be chosen—through constitutional processes that are set up in the constitution.[19]

By then, there were rumours in Jamaica that Sangster had been poisoned. Two-and-a-half years before, Ken Jones, the Minister of Communications and Works, had died from injuries he sustained when he fell from the balcony outside his bedroom at the Sunset Lodge Hotel in Montego Bay while he was attending a Cabinet retreat with his ministerial colleagues. Despite his wife's testimony at a coroner's inquest that he had been a sleepwalker and the decision by the inquest that he had fallen from the balcony because of this trait and his death was therefore due to misadventure,[20] rumours which had not yet been dispelled were that he had been pushed over the balcony by an envious colleague jealous of his national popularity. This view also intensified when the rumour factory said that Bustamante intended to carry out a major shake-up in the Cabinet at this retreat which would have seen Jones elevated to a more senior Cabinet post.

Memory of Jones' death was linked to Sangster's sudden incapacitation. The rumour escalated, gathering its own steam, and fueled by the public's ignorance of Sangster's medical history. In an attempt to counter the rumour, the Cabinet released a statement. It said:

> The Cabinet wishes the public to know that the doctors both in Montreal and in Jamaica have been very frank at all times about the Prime Minister's condition.
>
> The reports released by the Government have been complete and accurate and are not based on speculation or rumour, as would appear to be the case with some of the releases from certain other news sources.
>
> We are satisfied that the Prime Minister has had and continues to have the best medical care possible from a devoted team of doctors both here and in Montreal.[21]

The statement was broadcast on both radio stations in Jamaica and published in the press.

Sangster was knighted by Her Majesty the Queen while he was in a coma at the hospital on April 7, 1967.[22]

He died four days later.

He was prime minister for seven weeks and was incapacitated for the last three weeks of his life.

In an autopsy carried out by the doctors at the Montreal Neurological Hospital, a small (3mm) aneurysm of the anterior communicating artery was found. A pin-sized hole was present in the aneurysm. There was a clot around the aneurysm, the base of the brain, and intraventricularly. Widespread atherosclerosis was present in the carotid, vertebral and basilar arteries.[23]

As stated before, at the time of his death, and until now, there have been rumours of political mischief and that he had died from poisoning. The medical facts which have been outlined by Dr McNaughton, and his associates at the Montreal Neurological Institute, deny this completely. And when asked recently to comment on these rumours, Dr Herbert Eldemire's answer was one emphatic word: "Rubbish!" Essentially, Sangster suffered some of the complications of undertreated hypertension, cervic-cerebral atherosclerosis and intracranial hemorrhage, and he had an intracerebral aneurysm. A report on his final illness and his treatment by Dr John D. Stewart of the Montreal Neurological Institute, McGill University Health Centre and McGill University, insists that the diagnosis of SAH was correctly and promptly made by the physicians in Jamaica. Dr Stewart stated:

> Unfortunately, the carotid angiogram did not reveal the aneurysm; had it done so, early surgical clipping could have been performed and the outcome may possibly have been different. However, there was clearly an important degree of intracerebral vasospasm, a frequent and dangerous complication of SAH, and interestingly this was

misinterpreted as atherosclerosis by the neuroradiologist who was known to disbelieve the entity of post-SAH vasospasm, even though it had been described in 1951.

However, it is clear that the neurologists and neurosurgeons involved in Sangster's case were very familiar with this entity. Sangster's condition rapidly deteriorated to that of a grade 3 SAH (2) for which the prognosis at the time was grim; mortality rates have been gradually improving since then. The aggressive lowering of Sangster's elevated blood pressure, appropriate treatment by the standards of the day, has now been replaced by the very opposite: hypertension and volume expansion are the mainstays of treating post-SAH vasospasm.

Stewart's report was supported by Dr William Feindel (neurosurgeon and former director of the institute); Drs Renn Holness and David Sinclair (neurosurgeons); and Dr Leo Renaud (neurology resident working with Dr McNaughton during Sangster's final admission to the Montreal Neurological Institute).

A career which was just about to bloom and bear fruit had ended.

28 | OF THIS 'N THAT

In writing any biography, research often finds events involving the subject which do not necessarily fall in the stream of the story. Yet, they provide interesting aspects of the subject's life which give colour and substance and character portraits of the person which make them more interesting.

In the case of Donald Sangster, there was, for example, his athletic ability which continued long after he left Munro College. While he was articled to Mervyn T. King, the solicitor in Black River, he drove almost every morning to his old school to help the track team in their training. It also helped him to keep fit.

On his return home one morning he parked the car and went for a ride around the property on his horse. Not far from his home, he saw a cashew tree shaking and leaves and fruit falling to the ground. As he approached, a young boy about 14 years-old jumped from the tree and started to run. Sangster leaped from his horse and took after him. The boy was a fast runner, but Sangster was better at long-distance running and in due course caught up with the youngster.

"Young man," he said, "Why were you shaking the cashew tree?"

The boy was gasping, out of breath. "Well...sir...I...was..."

Sangster interrupted him, "When you shake the tree, in addition to the ripe fruit, young ones also fall. And that is a waste."

"True...sir...but...."

Again Sangster interrupted him.

> I tell you what. Here is two shillings. Use it to buy a crocus
> bag. Also, get a stick and a piece of wire. Tie the wire as a
> hook to the stick and use it to pick the ripe cashews. Carry

them in the bag to my house and give them to my mother
to make cashew stew. She'll give you some of it. You can also
spread out the cashew seeds on the barbecue to dry. Roast
and sell them to people driving on the road to Malvern and
Black River. Okay?

"Then you not going arrest me" the boy asked.

"Not this time."[1]

In later years, the boy—Samuel "Sammy" Lewis— became
a close friend of Sangster's.

During the next few days other boys in the district asked
him if they could also pick his cashews. And instead of the fruit
falling to the ground and rotting as before, these young men were
provided with an income. The boys also picked ackees and mangoes
during their season. His mother gave them some and sold the rest
to higglers. It was a rewarding deal for everyone.

One of the remembered qualities about him, which is still
spoken about by retired ministry of finance officials, is that when
he was the minister he had lunch quite often in the staff canteen.
One senior secretary recalls:

> He would arrive and look around for a seat. He would go to
> the table with the first empty seat he saw, and whether the
> other occupants were senior economists, budget analysts,
> drivers, messengers or clerks, he would walk to that table
> and sit. In the beginning, some members of the junior staff
> were uncomfortable with his presence, but he made them
> relax by discussing things in which they were interested.
> Cricket, of course, was his favourite subject. He was a great
> fan of Frank Worrell, for example, and they found he had no
> problem if they disagreed with him and argued that Everton
> Weekes was a better batsman.[2]

Dr Gladstone Bonnick who became a world bank consultant
subsequently, worked at the ministry of finance during the last
nine months of Sir Donald's life.

I was in a relatively junior position and had little personal contact with him. However, I do remember that before going abroad and immediately on returning he would put his head in each office to greet staff members. This warm personal touch helped to endear him to his staff. We respected him as an upright gentleman, untainted by the crude attributes associated with some of the politicians of the time.[3]

Jean Smith, a retired civil servant, was a family friend of Sangster's. When he first came to Kingston to live he boarded with her parents, Enos and Doris Jack on Collins Green Avenue in St Andrew. He kept in touch with the family over the years.

Shortly after he was appointed prime minister she was driving with her husband, Gerry, and they stopped at Andy Abraham's Texaco Service Station at the corner of Oxford and Old Hope Roads in Cross Roads, St Andrew. Sangster drove into the station and seeing them came out of the car and greeted them. Gerry Smith apologised that he had not yet congratulated him on his appointment, and wished him well. Sangster thanked him, and with a mischievous smile said, "Gerry, you and Jean are public servants, with permanent tenure. I am a politician and even as prime minister I am just a temporary clerk. The voters can fire me and my party at the next elections. My colleagues in the party can also vote to throw me out of office."

Tempus fugit!

Jean Smith has never forgotten those comments. During her time in the service she saw many politicians come into prominence with the glory of euphoria "and in the twinkle of an eye they were out in the cold".

There was a time, too, in England, Sangster was attending the 1966 Prime Minister's Conference and a book, *This Island Now* written by Peter Abrahams, the South African author who had become a Jamaican citizen immediately after Independence, had just been published. His press secretary purchased a copy, and after reading it he gave it to Sangster to read whenever he found the time.

This book is about an island, somewhere in the Caribbean, whose president dies. There is much mourning and the story tells of the death shortly after of his vice president who succeeded him. Abrahams then relates how one of the ministers in the Cabinet manipulates the news media, the civil service and the political directorate and takes over the government.

A week later, Sangster returned the book with this message: "Tell Peter, when we return to Jamaica, that he must not try to be a prophet."

On another occasion, Sangster was invited by Mayor of New York John Lindsay, to mount the Jamaica Coat of Arms on an archway over the Avenue of the Americas in New York City. He took the opportunity of doing so when he was traveling from Canada to Jamaica and stopped in New York City for the purpose.

Jamaica was then doing a special promotion of the musical form, 'ska', in the United States. The street was briefly closed for this event. The Jamaican Consulate in New York arranged for Byron Lee and the Dragonnaires and the singing group, the Blues Busters, who were involved in the promotion to perform at the function.

Thousands of people crowded the street and sidewalks. The Jamaicans in the crowd were dancing the ska and showing the Americans how it was done. Byron Lee had asked two young ladies from the consulate, Valerie Anderson and Patricia Latty to dance with the orchestra. Sangster and Lindsay were standing nearby, both snapping their fingers to the rhythm when the two ladies danced towards them. Valerie Anderson held Sangster's fingers and Patricia Latty held the hand of Lindsay. Both were pulled on to the streets for an impromptu "stage show". The crowd went wild. The television crews had a field day.

That night the main stories in the television news programmes were of Sangster and New York's mayor dancing on the streets of New York.

Afterwards, Sangster's Press Secretary went to the Consulate. Lance Evans, the Consulate's Information Officer had already written a pre-news release for transmission to the news media in Jamaica. He passed it to the Press Secretary who added a paragraph about the dancing. He then noticed that Evans had included about two paragraphs listing the names of some Jamaicans who were present at the function. He recognised only a few, and started crossing out the other names, calling them out to Evans and commenting they were not known in Jamaica. Evans looked a bit uncomfortable but said nothing; the Press Secretary was his senior and reported directly to the acting prime minister.

Looking towards the doorway by accident, the Press Secretary saw Sangster with his finger pressed to his lips and then signaling for the press secretary to join him. He did. They walked quickly away from the door along the corridor.

"Did you know the names you were crossing out of the release were in the room with you?" Sangster said.

Consternation!

"Leave it to me," he continued. You go back to the hotel. I'll tell Lance you had to leave urgently and that he should do what he thinks is okay with the story."

Further embarrassment was avoided. Later, the Press Secretary apologised profusely to Evans.[4] The lesson learned was that the officer on location knows more about the culture and the politics of his territory than temporary passers-by do.

Sangster often disarmed his opponents with his sense of humour. On one occasion, then Leader of the House Florizel Glasspole was smilingly instructed by the Speaker, B.B. Coke, not to describe his colleagues in the House as "gentlemen". During his speech, Glasspole had referred to "those gentlemen over there", pointing to members of the opposition. Coke immediately corrected him.

"The Honourable Leader of the House should not refer to members as gentlemen. They are 'members of this honourable House' and should be so addressed."[5]

The point was taken by Glasspole who then referred to them as "political angels".

Sangster was quick on his feet, asking the Speaker to permit this description "as it is a higher category".

He was, as has been pointed out before, very committed to the Commonwealth as an organization which could set an example of peoples of all races and all colours living together in peace and harmony. So when war broke out between Pakistan and India in 1965 over rival claims on Kashmir, he was very concerned about the damage it did to the image of the Commonwealth. The border clash also occurred during the Commonwealth Finance Ministers Conference taking place in Jamaica and over which he was presiding.[6]

The fighting threatened to engulf Asia and to involve other countries including Russia and China. He therefore offered his services to negotiate peace between the two countries. The offer was supported by members attending the conference. Happily, tempers cooled and there was a wave of relief through many world capitals at the belligerents' acceptance of a United Nations Security Council order for a ceasefire.[7]

Sangster was relieved. He sent a message to the ministers of finance of both countries expressing regret at their absence from the conference. He also expressed the relief of the members attending the conference at the ceasefire.

A friend subsequently asked what he thought he could have taken to the table to resolve the issue.

"Basically, he said, "it is the same, only on a larger scale, as two farmers who have been neighbours for years suddenly deciding to quarrel over where the fence between their properties should be. They really do not want to fight over it but they have to puff up—and as they say in the country—'go on bad'. And all they need is someone they trust to get them together and talk it over."

But suppose that did not work!

"I'd have arranged a two-match cricket tournament between the two, one match to be played in India and the other in Pakistan. Cricket is a healing sport," he chuckled.

It was Reverend Hugh Smythe, the rector of St Michael's Church who provided an insight into the spiritual side of Sangster's life and of what prayers meant to him. Smythe's father was rector of Gilnock and Santa Cruz in St Elizabeth and knew the family well. Reverend Smythe recalled:

> I first became acquainted with him when he was Lay Representative to the Synod, and this acquaintance was renewed in the late 1940s when I was rector of Balaclava.
>
> From then on, we have been in touch with each other. I knew him to be a man deeply interested in the church—he was mindful of its needs and he thought that the church should go hand in hand with the state, for indeed he believed in the fatherhood of God and the brotherhood of man. Although he was a member of the church in the country, whenever he had the opportunity of going to church in Kingston in a private capacity he would attend St Michael's.
>
> He would always ask me to pray for him. He would come to Holy Communion, taking his place in an unobtrusive manner with the other members of the congregation. Whenever he was under any strain or stress he never complained or said what the trouble was. He merely said, "Pray for me!"
>
> Before he left for the Prime Ministers' Conference in London last year, he came to see me at my home where I was sick in bed. He said he could not stay long, but he had

come to wish me a speedy recovery to health and asked me to pray for him.

After he was sworn-in as prime minister I telephoned to congratulate him. He asked me to pray for him and he promised to be in church on the Sunday morning after the motorcade. I expected him at the 7:00 a.m. service; he did not come but later sent an apology that he was so tired he could not get out of bed, but he would attend service on Easter Day.

We now know he was in hospital in Montreal on Easter Day.

On Monday, March 20, about two hours before he left for Canada, he sent for me. On arrival at Vale Royal at about 9:00 p.m., I was ushered into his room by one of his doctors. There he was lying on his bed but he stretched out his hand towards me and said: "It is so good of you to come pray for me."

I was with him for about half an hour until other doctors arrived. I told him I would see him later. He took my hand and said: "Thank you for the prayers." Later when he was taken downstairs I walked beside the stretcher and was by his side until the ambulance drove away. When in the ambulance, he took my hand again and repeated: "Thank you for the prayers. God bless you."[8]

Not long before his departure Sangster was visited by his son Anthony. His recollection of that night of his final meeting with his father is as clear as if it were yesterday.

Shortly after hearing the announcement on the radio that my father would be flown to Canada that very night for medical treatment, I made a telephone call to Vale Royal, his residence, to find out whether I would be able to visit him. I was put on to his close friend Andy Abrahams who said that it would not be possible, as he was not accepting visitors.

My fiancée's mother, seeing the look of disappointment and helplessness on my face turned to me and said, "If he were my father, I would have to see him." That comment gave me the courage and the determination to do something: I jumped in my car, an MG 1100 which, ironically, had been given to me by my father, and sped off to Vale Royal.

On arriving at Vale Royal, I got a message through to him that I was there, and not surprisingly, he was quite willing to see me. I went up to his bedroom where he lay on the bed, with various persons milling around, some of whom were helping to finalise the preparations for his departure. "Donald", as I tended to call him, greeted me warmly, held my hand, and made some complimentary remarks about my recent television appearances on the Jamaica Information Service's magazine evening programme. He was his usual jovial self and spoke coherently without any distortion. His face and neck looked flushed; but apart from that one would not have been able to detect that he was ill. I wished him a speedy recovery, said goodbye and left Vale Royal.

Little did I know, on leaving, that that was the last occasion on which I would see him alive. I am glad that I had persevered in my attempt to visit him, and cherish the memory of being by his bedside at that critical juncture of his life.

I am happy too that I was able over the next few weeks and down through the years to help quell the rumours that circulated across Jamaica about his death, particularly the one that said his skin had turned black (from poisoning) before he left the island, for Canada, on that fateful night.[9]

29 | THE LONG GOOD-BYE

Four hours after Sangster died, Hugh Shearer was sworn-in as the third prime minister of Jamaica.[1] His appointment marked the fourth time in 12 years that there were unexpected changes in the body politic of Jamaica.

The first of these changes began in 1955 when after being in office for ten years, the Jamaica Labour Party was defeated by the People's National Party in the general elections. Norman Manley became chief minister. Three years later, there were general elections for the Parliament of the Federation of the West Indies. Bustamante's party, the West Indies Democratic Party won these elections. The following year, Norman Manley called general elections in Jamaica, and won.

Two years later, however, there was a referendum to decide whether or not Jamaica should remain in the Federation. Manley and his party wanted Jamaica to continue in the Federation; Bustamante and his party wanted Jamaica to secede. Manley and the PNP lost.

Both political parties, therefore, decided to seek independence for Jamaica from Britain. This was granted and it was decided that Jamaica should become an independent nation on August 6, 1962.

Manley felt, however, that with such a significant constitutional change ahead for Jamaica, the people should be given the opportunity to decide which party they wished to lead them into independence. Elections were therefore held in April 1962, and the Jamaica Labour Party won.

So it was a political yo-yo for the people.

1967 came, and there was another series of movements of change. In February, Bustamante announced that because of ill health he would not contest the next elections which were about due, and he would resign as prime minister immediately the elections were held. Two months later there were elections. His party which was led by his deputy and the Acting Prime Minister Donald Sangster, won, and was appointed prime minister.

Seven weeks later, Sangster died. Four hours later, Hugh Shearer was appointed prime minister.

Jamaica's political stability was tested on both occasions. And Jamaica stood strong.

Tributes and messages of sorrow came from far and near. They came, from Her Majesty the Queen ("heartfelt sympathy to Sir Donald's colleagues, to the Government, and to my people in Jamaica, in their tragic loss"); the Governor-General Sir Clifford Campbell ("it is an irreparable loss to Jamaicans at this stage of our development, but God knows best"); Prime Minister Hugh Shearer ("his purpose was the building of a great Jamaica for his people"); Leader of the Opposition Norman Manley ("he was regarded with esteem and respect by all'); Sir Alexander Bustamante ("the country will miss him"); Lady Bustamante ("he will be greatly missed not only in the House of Representatives but outside as well"); and, from US President Lyndon B. Johnson; Canada's Prime Minister Lester Pearson; his recent guests the Prince and Princess of Monaco; Tanzanian President Julius Nyerere; the President of Malawi Kamusa Banda; the President of Venezuela Reinaldo Leandro Mora; the President of Zambia Kenneth Kaunda; and other Heads of Commonwealth countries; heads of international organizations, religious organizations and financial institutions.

In paying its tribute, the *Gleaner* noted:

> It is not that death is not our accepted common lot why the tragic end of Donald Burns Sangster has hit the nation (friend and foe alike) with such deep gloom. It was too unadvised, too sudden.
>
> Who could have thought that this man, not advanced

in years, thrifty of his energies except in national service, temperate in diet as in mood, could have been struck from amongst us before he could even fully assume his duties in the Cabinet? But such is the fate of man: betimes the fate of nations.

How many a land balanced in precarious struggle for rule could find itself thrown into chaos by such a stroke of fate! Happily for Jamaica, Sir Donald Sangster and his two pre-eminent predecessors in political leadership in Jamaica had set for long the pattern of orderly relationships in our Government and in the political machinery of the country.

Donald Burns Sangster scarce had time to charge his aide with the role of acting prime minister before semi-consciousness and coma intermittently overtook him in his fight for 22 days against the cerebral injury which had laid him low.

Donald Burns Sangster had come a long way in the public service before that sad day when his doctors took to the governor-general the news of his fiat for the man who was to act in his place. As a boy out of school, he tasted the ordeals of political service in his home parish of St Elizabeth where, before, his uncle —caustic and controversial—had been for a long time a noted legislator. Beaten but never bowed, defeated but never daunted, buffeted but never complaining— except for the characteristic shrug which became his talisman in diplomacy as well as in difficulty— Donald Sangster grew and grew in the service of his nation and his people.

As he grew under the shadow of that great and mighty leader of his party, Donald Sangster seemed often to be dwarfed by the flamboyant figure, drama and magical manner of his chief. Alongside other leaders he might not have appeared so humble—though modesty was of his essence. But alongside Sir Alexander Bustamante, even the most colourful of our other leaders would seem tame and prosaic by contrast. Yet the young tree grew in the political shade to strong roots and even stronger branches; it slowly took the stand to become at last the main pride and rallying point of the nation.

Everyone can visualise the struggle which beset the new prime minister as he took the full reins of office; premonitory signs may well have been occurring as his constitution shuddered at the strains. The dedication of a true public leader somehow never turns back from the crisis.

And so, Jamaica has lost in close fight a champion grim; in its parliament, a leader sage. He has gone clean and unsullied, as the poet said, with no cold gradations of decay as death broke the vital chain.[2]

His party/political opponent, Robert Lightbourne said that:

One of my greatest regrets would always be that Sir Donald had not taken all of his colleagues into his confidence with respect to a malady he had always lived with for the greater part of his life. There would have been even greater understanding between us, for the little mis-understandings of life are so often merely the result of ignorance.[3]

The night after his death, Sir Donald's body lay in state in the Christ Church Cathedral in Montreal from 9.00 to 11.00 p.m., in order to afford Jamaicans in Montreal as well as Canadian friends of Jamaica the opportunity of paying their last respects.

That night, a Royal Canadian Air Force Yukon transport plane provided by the Government of Canada brought the body to Montego Bay. On the flight were Senator Hector Wynter, minister of state, Vincent McFarlane, Jamaica's high commissioner to Canada, Dr Alfred Sangster, a cousin of Sir Donald, Ronald Kennedy, nephew-in-law, and Andy Abrahams and Clarence Chang, close personal friends of Sir Donald.

A period of mourning until Monday, April 17, was announced by the government. Half-masted flags, street corner groups, somber music by the radio stations and weeping citizens here and there were Kingston's first signs of mourning. The flags flew low on the poles of all government buildings, on business places, schools and at some private homes. People in groups at Constant Spring, Papine and through to downtown Kingston gathered and discussed the tragedy. The death of the Prime Minister dominated conversation at barber shops, bars, groceries, stores, supermarkets, and in homes and offices. Outside the Heywood Street market, a small crowd sang "Nearer My God to Thee".[4]

Across the lawn and behind the closed gates of Vale Royal, a cluster of household staff stood, and some sat motionless in the shadow of a solitary Jamaican Flag at half mast. And the Jamaica Philharmonic Symphony Orchestra dedicated its performance of Haydn's "Passion – the Seven Last Words" at the Ward Theatre that night to the memory of Sangster.

Over in Montego Bay, crowds started lining the waving gallery of the airport from the crack of dawn, awaiting the arrival of the body of the former prime minister. There was a notably subdued air among the people, conscious of the sadness of the occasion. On the ramp, officials of government, members of parliament, parliamentary secretaries, foreign representatives and local parish councillors, mayors and others began gathering, many with their wives.

Prime Minister Shearer arrived at 8.30 a.m. by a Jamaica Air Services aircraft, along with members of his Cabinet, and including Leader of the Opposition Norman Manley. A guard of honour, selected from the 1st Battalion of the Jamaica Regiment, and commanded by Major Leslie Lloyd, presented their usual smart appearance in rigid lines of scarlet coats and black trousers. Also present were Chief of Staff Brigadier David Smith, and Commissioner of Police Gordon Langdon.

Promptly at 9:00 a.m., the aircraft of the Royal Canadian Air Force touched down and taxied to a position on the left of the guard of honour. The casket was unloaded on the far side of the aeroplane and was received by pall bearers from the Jamaica Regiment. The flag-draped casket was then borne in slow march to a position in front of the guard of honour where the clergy of various churches awaited. These included the Rev. Philip Price, Archdeacon of Cornwall, the Rev. B.A.H. Jones of Holy Trinity Church, the Rev. M.L. Harrison, rector of the Parish Church, the Rev. Fr. D. Tobin, S.J. of the Church of the Blessed Sacrament, the Rev. F. Vipond of St Paul's United Church, and the Rev. David Yoh of St John's Methodist Church.[5]

When the casket was brought before it, the guard of honour presented arms while the clergy preceded the pall bearers to the hearse which stood by.

After the casket was loaded on to the hearse, the long cortege started slowly on its way to the Montego Bay railway station, preceded by an escort of police motorcycles along streets with sidewalks crowded with people. Mostly, they were silent, but every now and then a slight applause rippled through the air.

The casket was placed on a special funeral train. Slowly, it seemed reverently, the train with five coaches wended its way over the green hills of the Cockpit verges. People wept, holding black mourning flags in their hands. Black flags on bamboo poles on the tops of shops and houses fluttered sadly. It was a Thursday, not a Sunday; but both men and women wore their Sunday-best, the women in white dresses and white hats, the men in suits and hats which they took off and bowed their heads as the train went by. It was the same scene in Anchovy, Cambridge and Catadupa.

All eyes were on the third coach. It was open and painted in colours of black and white. In it was the casket, draped in the black, green and gold of the nation's flag. Five men of the Jamaica Regiment stood sentinel over it. Other coaches had the official mourning party of the Cabinet, members of Sir Donald's family, and other officials. The military bearers and guards for the cortege were in one coach. The police and members of the Press completed the sorrowing entourage.

The mournful procession stopped at Maggotty. There the casket was removed and taken by hearse to his birthplace, the tiny St Elizabeth village of Mountainside. This was where he grew his young years and it was appropriate that on this his last journey he should pass time with his own rural folk —the simple men and women with whom he had so much in common.

For six hours, from 3:00 p.m. to 9:00 p.m., his body lay in state in the Anglican Church where, as a boy, he went to Sunday School and learned the faith that was to remain with him throughout his full and eventful life. That night, all night, organists from churches in the parish, in relay, Messrs Warren, Jones, Evon Grant, Captain Johnson, Mrs Whittaker, Nurse Lawrence and Miss Roach filled the church with appropriate music. And while the thousands of St Elizabethans filed solemnly by the casket to take their last look at the prime minister, catechists and teachers in relay kept vigil in the sanctuary—B.B. Coke his political opponent for years, and Captain Cumberbatch, and Messrs Thompson, Crawford, Dunkley, Saams and Buchanan.

The following day, the casket was taken by the train to Chapelton where the body lay in state at the Anglican Church. It was then taken to Kingston the next day for the lying-in-state at the Kingston Parish Church in the afternoon, the Sunday and Monday.

Special prayers for the repose of his soul were included in the Sabbath Eve Service in the Synagogue on Duke Street in Kingston on Friday evening.[6] And, in an effort to identify the influences which shaped and moulded his character, RJR presented a documentary named, simply, "The Man from Mountainside". It was written by Peter Abrahams and produced by Howard Clarke. They traveled several hundreds of miles to obtain the voices they needed. Among these were Mrs Agnes Stathard who worked in the Sangster household at Mountainside and cared for the boy, Donald; Mrs Binger, the widow of the rector of Mountainside Church who preached to him; Easton Soutar, the deputy clerk of the Legislature, who helped to guide him in the Legislature when he was leader of the House; his brother Dudley Soutar who was his special assistant; and Pat Delapenha of Mandeville, a solicitor, a former PNP federal member of Parliament for the parish of Manchester, horticulturist and philanthropist, who knew him as a friend and colleague in young manhood.[7] Delapenha had represented him in the recount of the ballots in the 1947 parochial board elections.

Jamaica continued to pay homage to the late prime minister when his body was brought into Kingston at the end of a slow two-day journey across the island from Montego Bay.

The public lying-in-state started at 8.00 a.m. on Saturday, April 15 at the Kingston Parish Church. Almost immediately after the church was open, people started filing in; and, by degrees, the number grew. Throughout the day and into the evening, the two lines extended from the church, down King Street to Barry Street, turning into Barry Street and going into Temple Lane. The crowds kept coming during the whole day and policemen posted at strategic points were kept busy throughout, keeping the queues in order.

The casket bearing the body of Sir Donald lay in an area approaching the altar of the church. At the head were a cross of gold, and four large candles—two on either side—which threw a bright glow on the face of the dead prime minister. On the casket lay the insignia of the Knight Commander of the Royal Victorian Order which was awarded to him shortly before he died.

Five officers of the First Battalion of the Jamaica Regiment kept vigil at the coffin. Four were posted by the casket—one at each corner—and one stood apart. The scarlet and black ceremonial dress uniform of the guardsmen contrasted with the black and white of the casket.

The next day was the same. The crowds continued until Monday at noon when the lying-in-state ended. By then, the police estimated that over 100,000 persons passed to view the body.

Climaxing six days of national mourning which began when he died in Montreal, the state funeral on Monday afternoon was a massive tribute to the son of St Elizabeth who became his country's political head. In addition to the thousands who stationed themselves in downtown Kingston and the Victoria Park next door to the church, there were the tens of thousands who followed the impressive but melancholy ceremony on television and radio.

The service of thanksgiving in the historic Church of St Thomas the Apostle, better known as the Kingston Parish Church, was the focus of the nation's sorrow. The white-walled church, with its classic cruciform construction was filled to capacity when the peal of the organ signaled the entry of the procession of ministers for the start of the service. For half an hour before, the dignitaries and officials and mourners had been arriving—members of the cabinet, members of Parliament, the representatives of foreign governments, judges, civil servants, Custodes, mayors—the whole panoply of the body politic of Jamaica.

Under the high-ceilinged, white-painted dome of the church, the huge casket stood on a black catafalque. It was draped in the green, gold and black of the Jamaican flag. White lilies adorned stands placed near the bier, and massed in quiet beauty above the altar. Four tall, white candles in wooden holders, stood silent around the high catafalque. Near it, the Sangster family, heavy with grief, sat in a special place of honour.

Outside, the crowd crammed the northern side of South Parade, facing the church. The gun-carriage, which was to head the cortege in the procession through the streets of Kingston, was drawn-up in readiness. And, at East Parade, the guard of honour of the first battalion of the Jamaica Regiment waited, their scarlet tunics making a vivid splash of colour in the bright afternoon sun.

Inside the church, the soft notes of the organ crept into the silence of the waiting mourners. The purple-gowned choristers took their places. The church bell mounted high in its tall tower above the building began a mournful tolling. And so, the majesty and the glory of Donald Sangster's funeral began as the hands of the clock moved towards 3:00 p.m. for the start of the service.

Ritual and ceremonial were combined. The traditional Twenty-third Psalm gave its message of faith and hope. Prime Minister Shearer read the first lesson from Revelations, in which John the Divine spoke of the promise of after-life. Canon R.O.C. King eloquently expressed the nation's praise for its noble departed son. Prayers were said for those who had gone, and for those who mourned. Time-honoured funeral hymns were sung.

After the singing of the first verse of the Jamaican National Anthem, the cortege moved out of the church to the sad music of Handel's "Dead March". The casket was borne by the red-coated soldiers to the gun carriage. The serious-faced cabinet ministers took up position on either side of the casket; and the cortege started its slow procession, with the drums of the massed bands repeating the mournful theme of the "Dead March". Beginning, too, was the salute of 56 guns, one for each year of his life, at one-minute intervals.

Along East Queen Street and then up Duke Street the cortege went. And it was fitting that Donald Sangster would make his last journey through Kingston on a street that played such a significant role in his life. He passed Headquarters House and Gordon House, honoured scenes of his parliamentary career. He passed the headquarters of the Bustamante Industrial Trade Union with which he was close in his lifetime. And he passed Melrose Hotel, where for many years he lived a simple bachelor's life.

As the cortege passed Gordon House, a great wail went up from some of the women mourners massed on the sidewalk. These were the heart-cries of sorrow from a grief-stricken nation that these emotional women were not ashamed to vent openly.

Then the scene shifted to the George VI Memorial Park, in which the Cabinet recently designated an area adjacent to the National Shrine reserved for National Heroes, as the final resting place for Jamaican prime ministers.

The casket was borne to a central position beneath a cluster of tall, green willows.

He became the first Jamaican prime minister to be laid to rest there.

And the last, sad, final rites were said.

The casket bearing the remains of Sir Donald is taken from the Church of St Thomas the Apostle (Kingston Parish Church) for final resting place at the George VI Memorial Park, later renamed National Heroes Park.

Family members on the day of the funeral of Sir Donald Sangster. Standing from left to right, Derrick Sangster, Mrs Ray Kennedy, Bindley Sangster, Cecil Sangster, Iris Sangster and Ferdinand Sangster.

Photographs ©The Gleaner Company

30 | HIS MEMORIALS

Memorial services were held for Donald Sangster at Westminster Abbey in London, the Anglican Cathedral of Christ Church in Montreal, the Anglican Cathedral in Birmingham, the Willesden Baptist Church in London, the Holy Trinity Cathedral in Port-of-Spain in Trinidad, and the Washington Cathedral in Washington D.C. At the latter, the eulogy was delivered by US Secretary of Labour W. William Wirtz. He described the legacy of Sangster as that "in living, he ennobled his office with his humanity". Among the many memorial services held in Jamaica were those at the Church of St Margaret in Liguanea, St Andrew, the Watermount Baptist Church in St Catherine, the Bethlehem Baptist Church, Rock River, Clarendon, and the Parish Church in St Ann's Bay, St Ann. Memorial services were also held at the Anglican Cathedral in Port-of-Spain, Trinidad. There was also a memorial service at St Mark's Church, Kensington in London held by the Friends of the Jamaica Labour Party in London on May 7.

The United Nations flag at the headquarters of the world organization was flown at half-mast, and national flags were also flown at half-mast in Trinidad & Tobago and Barbados.

Jamaica's radio commentaries of the funeral were beamed to other parts of the Caribbean and to London in collaboration with Cable and Wireless (W.I.) Ltd. The JBC's commentary was carried by the Windward Islands Broadcasting Service emanating from Grenada, and covering the French Caribbean. The RJR commentary was made available to Barbados and Guyana.[1]

Poems about Sir Donald were written by people and sent to the newspapers for publication. Well-known poet, Inez Knibb Sibley's poem was one. It said:

> While time was yours – and endless zest
>
> You burnt the midnight oil!
>
> Spent all your days
>
> In tireless thinking. Planning
>
> Devious ways
>
> To add to nation's good, subtract from need.
>
> For love of nation was your creed
>
> And love of home – JAMAICA'S SON.
>
> Your epitaph now is "SERVICE"
>
> Your sure reward, "Well done".

Another was an acrostic by Troy Caine, a student at Munro College, the first letter of each line spelling the name "SIR DONALD SANGSTER".

> **S**o fair and vivacious your bright fame shone
>
> **I**n our blessed isle and in foreign lands,
>
> **R**ising to the apex of value with courage, for
>
> **D**eeds fully stablished you noble – a loyal son
>
> **O**f our dear country. With skilled hands
>
> **N**ational pride was carved, and like a bright star
>
> **A**lways radiating its illumined vigour, you sparked,
>
> **L**oving the ideals of truth, of honesty, and of honour.
>
> **D**eeds of wisdom and knowledge were achieved
>
> **B**y you, Sir Donald – your noble aims marked
>
> **U**tmost talent, and in your attitude and manner
>
> **R**ose magnificence by which we were not deceived.
>
> **N**ow so low you lay, silenced to the blessed tale
>
> **S**o much you loved, cut off from the glory that

Steered you up just yesterday to powerful splendour,

All our griefs are spent, yet for just a while

None of us knew death lurked where you sat.

Gone from us is a noble heart, a man of wonder,

Struggling for our problems that made him still.

Though we mourn you, dear leader, never shall we cease

Endeavouring to remember you; and we now hope you will

Rest eternally in Heaven's glory and peace.

There was also a poem, "In remembrance" written by 11-year-old Christopher Harris:

Oh Fellowmen of Jamaica now grieved, we say

That our Prime Minister is dead – but let us pray

For his soul to rest in peace,

And many more men like him increase.

As Prime Minister one only month he spent,

A faithful server of our Government

He fought for his people, and our Island's pride,

For he ever had God as his guide.

Suggestions for memorials came from all over Jamaica, including one from Ivan Delevante, a businessman, who wanted Washington Boulevard in St Andrew to be renamed "Sangster Boulevard", and that the Palisadoes Airport to be re-named the "Sangster International Airport". Another was from the Matron of the Savanna-la-Mar Infirmary Ms L. Heron Parkes, who suggested a neurological wing at the University of the West Indies, or a ward at the Black River or Chapelton Hospitals to be named after him. She and the staff donated five guineas to start the fund. It was a national outpouring of love and affection.

He had been described by *Spotlight* magazine two years earlier as one who was approachable yet firm.

He has created the image of a trustworthy man who with full power would hold the scales more evenly. He is not among the Party's splashers in the spoils system.... Respect begets respect, and the records of the Legislature have yet to show a biting venomous speech by him. In many a bitter debate he has been the mellowed mediator between tart-tongued floor MPs and even some ministers and front bench opposition members. In electioneering party politics he is also no slush-slasher. This clean quality has kept his integrity stocks high among the community as a whole.

A final tribute to his predecessor was made in a radio and television broadcast the day after the funeral by Prime Minister Hugh Shearer:

> Today I met with my Cabinet. Before we started our meeting I invited the Lord Bishop of Jamaica, the Right Reverend Dr Percival Gibson, to join with us, and he was kind enough to ask for God's blessing in guiding us in our counsels, and that He would always be with us in our deliberations for the good of Jamaica and Jamaicans.
>
> At the end of our prayers we began our discussions, but all the while we kept remembering this man, who only two short months ago had chosen us as his Cabinet team and had left us suddenly to carry out the work to which he had dedicated himself; and he had hoped to do.
>
> The first task we set ourselves was to discuss the manner in which we could honour his memory in perpetuity. And we have decided on five memorials.
>
> The first is to name the new Income Tax Office now being built on East Street in Kingston, "The Sir Donald Sangster Building". This is the newest, most modern and most impressive Government office in Jamaica and it stands out as a monument to his work as minister of finance.
>
> The second is that the Montego Bay International Airport will now be called the 'Sangster International Airport'. Sir Donald was an international figure and this airport at which

so many world-famous persons land daily will be a reminder forever of his stature in the world.

The third is to issue a commemorative stamp. This will be the first time that a Jamaican issue of stamps will carry a portrait of the prime minister of this country.

We have also decided to launch a fund which will be called the Sir Donald Sangster Memorial Fund. A Select Committee will be established, which in consultation with the Government and members of the family will determine its appropriate use.

To start this fund, I have donated One Hundred Pounds and my Cabinet colleagues have donated Fifty Pounds each. Sir Alexander Bustamante and Lady Bustamante have also informed me that they will contribute the sum of Two Hundred Pounds, and I now appeal to you all to support it.

As you know, too, we decided last week to invite you to submit designs for a suitable mausoleum to be erected at the site where Sir Donald was buried yesterday.[2]

Later in the year, a resolution was proposed by the Clarendon Parish Council that government should create a national public holiday each year on Sangster's birthday.

A year later, the Half Moon Rose Hall Club in Montego Bay, St James launched a golf competition to honour Sangster's memory. He played golf whenever he could find the time. The trophy, a Silver Bowl was named the "Sir Donald Sangster Memorial Trophy", to be competed for each year on February 22. Sir Donald had opened the golf course by driving on January 5, 1964, and he was an honorary member of the club. The Postal Department also issued two memorial stamps. They were in the 3d and 1/6d denominations.

The mausoleum was designed by Moystyn Campbell, chief architect of the Ministry of Works. The Sir Donald Sangster

Memorial Library was built in Chapelton from funds launched by Hugh Shearer, and his portrait is printed on the One Hundred Dollar note.

Another memorial was a long-playing record produced for the Jamaica Information Service by Carey Robinson. The recording included tributes by Prime Minister Hugh Shearer, Opposition Leader Norman Manley, Florizel Glasspole who subsequently became governor-general, Canon R.O.C. King, sports administrator Herbert McDonald, and former RJR's sportscaster Roy Lawrence, and reminiscences by a retired Munro College caretaker, and excerpts from Sangster's speeches. It also included a poem read by a Jamaica Information Service television producer, Audrey Chong.[3]

Four years after his death, a resolution was moved by the St Elizabeth Parochial Board asking the government to erect an appropriate and suitable monument to his memory in the parish. In addition, a resolution was circulated to all parish councils for the government to declare a public holiday on the anniversary of his birth. However, neither of these proposals was carried through.

Recently, a committee has been working towards the setting up of a Sir Donald Sangster Trust Fund. Members are Anthony Johnson, Mrs Hope Sangster, Bindley Sangster, Anthony Falloon and the Hon. Dr Alfred Sangster. Among the objectives of the Trust will be to award a scholarship to Munro College in St Elizabeth which he attended and to Clarendon College in Chapelton, Clarendon, which was the high school in his last constituency.[4]

What made this man what he was? He did not fly a flag of his achievements. These spoke for themselves. He played politics as if it were a game of cricket. To him it was not how one won the game but how one performed as a sportsman, enjoying success without boasting and not crying or blaming others for losses.

He knew no hate. He hoped others would forgive his transgressions. No one believed more in the philosophy of peace and love than he did.

The lessons he learned as a boy guided him all his life. The Bible his mother gave him were the last words he read before he fell asleep. He praised God for his glory and believed in the power of prayer. He enjoyed music, art, the theatre, the dance, movies and sports because they appealed to body and soul and gave to life dimensions beyond length and breadth, and height and depth.

He was a special man.

Yet, while he was recognised as a world leader when he died, his memory was short-lived in Jamaica. Hugh Shearer, his successor as prime minister announced four memorials:

(1)   A competition for the design of a mausoleum to be constructed at the site at which he was buried in National Heroes Park. This design was done by Moystyn Campbell, the chief architect of the Public Works Department. It was built one year later—the Income Tax Department's Head Office on East Street was named the 'Donald Sangster Memorial Building'. This was done shortly after his death, but without any public ceremony;

(2)   The airport in Montego Bay was to be renamed the 'Sangster International Airport' This, however, involved informing airport authorities, airlines and other organizations involved in the aviation industry worldwide, and was not finalised until 1972. And, although a sign was mounted at the airport indicating its new name, it was almost 20 years later that a plaque was displayed there to identify who he was.

(3)   Two special memorial stamps —a three pence and a one shilling and six pence stamp—were issued four months after he died, and were on sale at post offices for three months. Today, except for stamp collectors and members of his family who have them in their possession, these stamps are no where to be found. As memorials they have been forgotten.

(4)   The construction of a public library in Chapelton, Clarendon in the constituency he was serving when he died. This building was not completed until 19 years later and officially opened to the public on June 6, 1988.

Subsequently, his portrait was printed on the $100 currency note issued by the Bank of Jamaica on December 1, 1986. The note is popularly known as a "Sangster", but who he was is not widely known by the young people of today.

In the meanwhile, following the deaths of Norman Manley, Alexander Bustamante and Michael Manley, annual tributes have been paid to their memories. None, however, were held for Sangster. This was only done just before the general elections in 2007, when ceremonials were held at his last resting place in National Heroes Park in Kingston, and in Chapelton, Clarendon, the last constituency he served.

Donald Sangster has been, indeed, the forgotten prime minister.

Sangster International Airport, Montego Bay, Jamaica

Three-Pence Commemorative stamp bearing the portrait of Sir Donald Sangster.

The Sir Donald Sangster Building, former home of Jamaica's Income Tax Office at 116 East Street, Kingston.

DONALD SANGSTER — A CHRONOLOGY

1911   Born October 26, at Victoria Jubilee Hospital, Kingston, to Cassandra and William Sangster of Fullerswood, St Elizabeth

1921-1929   Attended Munro College. Outstanding at athletics, cricket and academics. Came second in Jamaica in Senior Cambridge Examinations, 1927

c.1930   Articled to lawyer, Mervyn T. King, at Black River. Also studied bookkeeping and accounting

1933   Elected to St Elizabeth Parochial Board.

1937   First in the island in final solicitor's exams. Opened law practices in Black River and Santa Cruz

1941   Elected Vice Chairman of St Elizabeth Parochial Board

1944   Contested South St Elizabeth seat as an independent in Jamaica's first election under universal adult suffrage, and lost

1949   Elected chair of the St Elizabeth Parochial Board. Won South St Elizabeth seat as JLP candidate; became Minister of Social Welfare; Premier Bustamante appointed him First Deputy Leader

1953   Became Minister of Finance and Leader of the House of Representatives on the death of Sir Harold Allan

1955   January—lost seat in general election which brought the PNP to power; opened law office in Kingston. December—won North East Clarendon seat in a by-election. Appointed by Bustamante Opposition Spokesman on Finance and party's chief spokesman on preparations for the West Indies Federation

1961 Jamaica voted against Federation in Referendum. Sangster appointed to committee to draw up a new constitution for an independent Jamaica

1962 April 10, JLP won election; Sangster returned as Minister of Finance; Appointed chairman of consultative committee on Independence

1963 Appointed Deputy Prime Minister

1965 His health failing, Bustamante appointed Sangster Acting Prime Minister, Acting Minister of External Affairs, Acting Minister of Defence

1966 Sangster flown to Montreal Neurological Institute for health check

1967 Led by Sangster, JLP won election

February 21, Sangster became Prime Minister

March 18, suffered cerebral seizure while on retreat at Newcastle preparing for the Budget

March 21, flown to Montreal Neurological Institute

April 7, Knighted by the Queen while in a coma

April 11, died in hospital in Montreal. Hugh Shearer sworn in as Jamaica's third Prime Minister

April 17, interred at National Heroes Park after State Funeral

BIBLIOGRAPHY

The Daily Gleaner
Public Opinion
Spotlight magazine
Newday magazine
The Voice
West Indian Economist
Senior, Olive. *Encyclopedia of Jamaican Heritage*. Kingston: Twin Guinep Publishers, 2003
Jamaica Information Service
Gleaner Geography and History of Jamaica. 23rd edition. Kingston. The Gleaner, 1995
Eaton, George. *Alexander Bustamante and Modern Jamaica*, Kingston Publishers, 1975
The Parliamentarians – History of the Commonwealth Parliamentary Association, 1911-1985
Hill, Frank. *Bustamante and his Letters*. Kingston: Kingston Publishers, 1976
Working Together for Development – D.T.M. Girvan. Compiled and edited by Norman Girvan
The Memoirs of Lady Bustamante, ed Leeta Hearne, Kingston: Kingston Publishers, 1998
Who's Who in Jamaica (during the 1950s and 1960s)
Handbook of Jamaica, 1944, 1950, 1960, 1962, 1967
Chronicle of the 20th Century – Dorling Kindersley Limited, 9 Henrietta Street, London WC2E 8PS
Crisis in Africa, Arthur Gavshon, Pelican Books, African Affairs, Editor, Ronald Segal
John Roby: Members of the Assembly of Jamaica from the institution of that branch of the Legislature to the present time – 1831-1837
The Jamaican People: 1880-1902 by Patrick Bryan – Warwick University Caribbean Series
Guide to Jamaica, Phillip P. Olley

NOTES

Preface

1. In order to inform how the Legislature worked, the author referred to members of the Jamaican Assembly from the institution of that branch of the Legislature to the present time—1831-1837, John Roby

2. For the 1944 General Elections, the Jamaica Labour Party (JLP) had contested 29 of the 32 seats, and the Peoples National Party (PNP) 19. Within six months, recounts and changes in seat standings changed the final numbers in the House—clarification as provided by Troy Caine, political historian

Chapter 1

1. Author's note—Bustamante and Norman Manley were first cousins; Hugh Shearer was a relative on both their mothers' side; Michael Manley was Norman's son

2. Information on other parliamentarians mentioned is obtained from the *Handbooks of Jamaica, 1944 to 1971*

Chapter 2

1. From the family history kept by Dr the Hon. Alfred Sangster, O.J.

2. Interview with Alicia Sangster, cousin of Sir Donald Sangster, December 27, 2006

3. Interview with Alicia Sangster

4. From the Will of William Burns Sangster, recorded November 4, 1927, Supreme Court Will Book 22, Folio 351 (Source: B0067 Jamaica Supreme Court Wills 1924, 1926-1930.)

5. *Bustamante and his Letters*, Frank Hill—Kingston Publishers

6. Interview with George Davis of Mountainside

7. Biographical notes from the Jamaica Information Service – *Facts on Jamaica No. 18*

8. *Encyclopedia of Jamaican Heritage* by Olive Senior. Twin Guinep Publishers

Chapter 3

1. *Daily Gleaner*, April 18, 1967
2. Handbook of Jamaica 1962
3. *The Munronian*, 1924
4. *The Munronian*, 1927
5. *History of the Inter-Secondary Schools Championship Sports*, Sir Herbert McDonald
6. *The Munronian*, 1929
7. *History of the Inter-Secondary Schools Championship Sports*, Sir Herbert McDonald
8. *The Munronian*, 1928
9. *The Munronian*, 1928
10. *The Munronian*, 1928
11. *The Munronian*, 1949
12. *Daily Gleaner*, June 24, 1949
13. Interview with Ken Parchment, member of the St Elizabeth Nethersole Cup Parish Cricket Team, of which Sangster was captian
14. The Sir Donald Sangster papers and documents at the National Library of Jamaica
15. The Sir Donald Sangster papers and documents at the National Library of Jamaica
16. Interview with Dr Alfred Sangster
17. Interview with Dr Alfred Sangster
18. Interview with Dr Alfred Sangster
19. *Jamaican Leaders*, Anthony Johnson

Chapter 4

1. The Sir Donald Sangster collection of papers, documents, photographs, etc., at the National Library of Jamaica
2. Interview with Dr Alfred Sangster
3. *Jamaican Leaders*, Anthony Johnson
4. Interview with Mrs. Joyce Francis
5. Interviews with Caswell Green, whose property adjoined Sangster's Fruitfield property, and with Sammy Lewis, another Mountainside resident
6. Interview with George Davis

7. Interview with Sammy Lewis, Caswell Green and other Mountainside residents
8. Interview with Dr the Hon. Joyce Robinson
9. Interview with Caswell Green
10. *Daily Gleaner*, March 9, 1939, p. 21
11. *Facts on Jamaica No. 18* – Biographical notes, Jamaica Information Service
12. *Jamaican Leaders*, Anthony Johnson
13. *Daily Gleaner*, April 12, 1967, p.14
14. Interview with Ken Parchment recalling a 1949 conversation with Donald Sangster
15. *Daily Gleaner*, November 12, 1944
16. Interview with Lee Binns, a consultant on craft and information in the book, *Working Together for Development*, compiled by Norman Girvan

Chapter 5
1. Recollections by Donald Sangster's son, Bindley Sangster, 2006
2. *Daily Gleaner*, April 2, 1958
3. *The Voice*, April 1, 1961, p. 1
4. *Daily Gleaner*, April 26, 1960
5. *Daily Gleaner*, May 11, 1960

Chapter 6
1. *Spotlight* magazine, December 1949
2. *Spotlight* magazine, February 1951, p. 12; and *Daily Gleaner*, January 13, 1951
3. *Jamaican Leaders*, Anthony Johnson

Chapter 7
1. *Daily Gleaner*, August 5, 1951
2. *Spotlight* magazine, June 1951, p. 18
3. *Spotlight* magazine, June 1951, p. 18

Chapter 8
1. *Daily Gleaner*, May 27, 1953
2. *Spotlight* magazine, November 1954, p. 25
3. *Spotlight* magazine, December 1953, p. 19
4. *Spotlight* magazine, May 1954, p. 17
5. *Spotlight* magazine, December 1954, p. 21

Chapter 9
1. *Spotlight* magazine, April 1955, p. 20
2. *Spotlight* magazine, April 1955, p. 21
3. *Spotlight* magazine, November 1955, p. 15, p. 21
4. From the Sir Donald Sangster papers and documents deposited at the National Library of Jamaica
5. *The Voice*, August 10, 1957, p. 2
6. Interview with Madge Broderick, daughter of P.W. Broderick
7. *The Voice*, August 29, 1959, p. 8
8. *The Voice*, September 12, 1959, p. 6
9. *The Voice*, September 9, 1961, p. 7
10. *The Voice*, June 20, 1964, p. 5
11. *The Voice*, July 15, 1961
12. *The Voice*, October 15, 1960
13. *Daily Gleaner*, November 15, 1960, and *The Voice*, November 5, 1960 and January 7, 1961
14. *Daily Gleaner*, January 22, 1961 and *The Voice*, January 28, 1961

Chapter 10
1. *Newday* magazine, June-July 1960
2. *Newday* magazine, June-July 1960

Chapter 11
1. *Daily Gleaner*, February 2, 1962. Also, *Daily Gleaner*, October 12, 1961
2. *The Voice*, February 10, 1962
3. *The Voice*, February 17, 1962, p. 1

Chapter 12
1. *Daily Gleaner*, May 5, 1963
2. *Daily Gleaner*, June 14, 1962
3. *Daily Gleaner*, April 4, 1962
4. *Daily Gleaner*, May 2, 1962
5. *Daily Gleaner*, June 7, 1962
6. *Daily Gleaner*, June 22, 1962

Chapter 13
1. *Daily Gleaner*, June 21, 1962
2. *Daily Gleaner*, June 28, 1962 and *The Voice*, June 30, 1962
3. *Daily Gleaner*, June 28, 1962
4. *Daily Gleaner*, July 1, 1962
5. *Daily Gleaner*, July 2, 1962
6. *Daily Gleaner*, July 2, 1962

Chapter 14
1. Jamaica Information Service files
2. *Daily Gleaner*, June 15, 1962
3. *Daily Gleaner*, July 22, 1962
4. *Daily Gleaner*, September 9, 1962
5. *Daily Gleaner*, May 9, 1962 and *The Voice*, May 12, 1962
6. *The Voice*, June 1, 1962 and *Daily Gleaner*, May 31, 1962
7. *The Voice*, July 28, 1962 and *Daily Gleaner*, July 24, 1962
8. *Daily Gleaner*, October 31, 1962 and *The Voice*, November 3, 1962
9. *Daily Gleaner*, October 19, 1962 and *The Voice*, October 20, 1962
10. *The Voice*, November 11, 1962

Chapter 15
1. *Daily Gleaner*, March 12, 1963 and *The Voice*, March 16, 1963
2. *Daily Gleaner*, April 11, 1963
3. *Daily Gleaner*, May 29, 1963, p. 9
4. *Daily Gleaner*, April 11, 1963, p. 14
5. *Daily Gleaner*, April 11, 1963
6. *Daily Gleaner*, July 25, 1963
7. *Daily Gleaner*, November 8, 1963
8. *Daily Gleaner*, December 10, 1963

Chapter 16

1. *Daily Gleaner*, April 1, 1964
2. *The Voice*, April 11, 1964, p. 1
3. *The Voice*, April 25, 1964, p. 1; *Daily Gleaner*, April 23, 1964
4. *The Voice*, June 12, 1964
5. *Spotlight* magazine, July 1965, p. 10
6. *The Voice*, September 19, 1964, p. 1
7. *Daily Gleaner*, October 22, 1964 and *Spotlight* magazine, October 1964

Chapter 17

1. *The Voice*, November 7, 1964
2. *Daily Gleaner*, November 5, 1964
3. *The Voice*, November 14, 1964
4. *The Parliamentarians: History of the Commonwealth Parliamentary Association, 1911-1985*, 1994, Ian Grey
5. *Daily Gleaner*, November 17, 1964 and *The Voice*, November 21, 1964
6. *Daily Gleaner*, November 17, 1964
7. *Daily Gleaner*, September 23, 1965

Chapter 18

1. *Spotlight* magazine – February/March 1966, p. 6
2. *Daily Gleaner*, April 22, 1966
3. *Garvey and Garveyism*, Amy Jacques Garvey. Collier Books, 866 First Avenue, N.Y., N.Y. 10026
4. *The Autobiography of Una Marson*, by Una Marson
5. *Daily Gleaner*, July 31, 1950
6. *Daily Gleaner*, March 25, 1954
7. *Daily Gleaner*, April 28, 1954
8. *Daily Gleaner*, June 4, 1961
9. *Daily Gleaner*, June 3, 1961
10. *Daily Gleaner*, August 5, 1961
11. *Daily Gleaner*, October 27, 1961
12. *Daily Gleaner*, March 20, 1962
13. *Daily Gleaner*, April 25, 1966
14. *Daily Gleaner*, April 22, 1966, p. 1
15. *Daily Gleaner*, May 7, 1966, p. 1

Chapter 19
1. *Daily Gleaner*, November 21, 1966
2. *Daily Gleaner*, January 5, 1967

Chapter 20
1. *Daily Gleaner*, March 27, 1966
2. *Daily Gleaner*, April 15, 1966 and *The Voice*, April 16, 1966
3. *Daily Gleaner*, January 20, 1966, p. 1
4. *The Voice*, July 16, 1966
5. *The Voice*, September 24, 1966
6. *Daily Gleaner*, April 9, 1965
7. *Daily Gleaner*, September 21, 1966 and *The Voice*, September 24, 1966
8. *Daily Gleaner*, June 28, 1966 and *The Voice*, July 2, 1966

Chapter 21
1. *Daily Gleaner*, August 9, 1963
2. *Daily Gleaner*, July 2, 1959
3. *Daily Gleaner*, July 4, 1959
4. *Daily Gleaner*, September 30, 1965
5. Daily Gleaner, September 19, 21, 22 and October 3, 1956
6. *Daily Gleaner*, January 7, 1966 and The Voice, January 8, 1966
7. *Daily Gleaner*, January 8, 1966 and The Voice, January 15, 1966
8. *Daily Gleaner*, January 14, 1966
9. *Daily Gleaner*, September 7, 1966 and *The Voice*, September 3, 1966
10. *Daily Gleaner*, September 6, 1968
11. *The Voice*, September 17, 1966 and *Jamaican Leaders*, Anthony Johnson

Chapter 22
1. Conversation with Carmen Gauntlett, one of Prime Minister Alexander Bustamante's secretaries
2. *Daily Gleaner*, June 28, 1962
3. *Daily Gleaner*, June 24, 1966
4. *Daily Gleaner*, October 4, 1966
5. *Daily Gleaner*, March 17, 1965
6. Conversation with Hector Wynter, circa 2000
7. *Daily Gleaner*, November 27, 1966
8. *Daily Gleaner*, February 28, 1967
9. *Daily Gleaner*, March 1, 1967

Chapter 23

1. *Daily Gleaner*, January 3, 1967
2. *Daily Gleaner*, January 3, 1967
3. *Daily Gleaner*, January 1, 1967
4. *Daily Gleaner*, January 3, 1967
5. *Daily Gleaner*, January 1, 1967
6. *Daily Gleaner*, January 9. 1967
7. *Daily Gleaner*, January 13, 1967
8. *Daily Gleaner*, January 11, 1967
9. *Daily Gleaner*, January 20, 1967 and *Spotlight* magazine, January 1967
10. *Daily Gleaner*, January 12, 1967
11. *Daily Gleaner*, January 14, 1967
12. *Daily Gleaner*, January 18, 1967, p. 1
13. *Daily Gleaner*, January 18, 1967
14. *Daily Gleaner*, January 19, 1967
15. *Daily Gleaner*, January 21, 1967
16. *Daily Gleaner*, January 21, 1967
17. *Daily Gleaner*, January 24, 1967
18. *Daily Gleaner*, January 25, 1967
19. *Daily Gleaner*, January 25, 1967

Chapter 24

1. *Daily Gleaner*, January 26, 1967
2. *Daily Gleaner*, January 24, 1967
3. *Daily Gleaner*, February 7, 1967
4. *Daily Gleaner*, January 26, 1967, p. 1
5. *Daily Gleaner*, February 11, 1967
6. *Daily Gleaner*, January 25, 1967
7. *Daily Gleaner*, February 2, 1967
8. *Daily Gleaner*, February 4, 1967
9. *Daily Gleaner*, February 7, 1967
10. *Daily Gleaner*, February 12, 1967
11. *Daily Gleaner*, February 11, 1967
12. *Daily Gleaner*, January 29, 1967

13. Conversation between the author of this biography and the late Gloria Lannaman, former general manager of the Jamaica Broadcasting Corporation (date unavailable)
14. *Daily Gleaner*, February 15, 1967
15. *Daily Gleaner*, February 16, 1967
16. *Daily Gleaner*, February 21, 1967
17. *Daily Gleaner*, February 22, 1967
18. *Daily Gleaner*, February 22, 1967
19. *Daily Gleaner*, March 4, 1967
20. *Daily Gleaner*, February 23, 1967
21. *Daily Gleaner*, February 24, 1967
22. Personal reminiscences by the author of this biography, who was Donald Sangster's press secretary

Chapter 25
1. *Daily Gleaner*, February 23, 1967

Chapter 26
1. *Daily Gleaner*, February 28, 1967
2. *Daily Gleaner*, March 1, 1967 and *The Voice*, March 4, 1967
3. *Daily Gleaner*, March 1, 1967
4. *Daily Gleaner*, March 4, 1967
5. Extracts from report of Canadian doctors who treated Sir Donald Sangster at the Montreal Neurological Institute, 1967
6. *Daily Gleaner*, March 7, 1967
7. *Daily Gleaner*, January 28, 1967
8. *Daily Gleaner*, March 4, 1967
9. *Daily Gleaner*, March 9, 1967
10. *Daily Gleaner*, March 14, 1967
11. *Daily Gleaner*, March 16, 1967
12. *Daily Gleaner*, March 16, 1967
13. *Daily Gleaner*, March 16, 1967
14. *Daily Gleaner*, March 19, 1967
15. The medical statements are from a report by Dr John Stewart of the Montreal Neurological Institute, provided to Dr Alfred Sangster, 2002

Chapter 27

1. The medical statements in this chapter are from reports by Dr Francis McNaughton and Dr John Stewart of the Montreal Neurological Institute, provided to Dr Alfred Sangster, 2002
2. *The Voice*, March 25, 1967, p. 1
3. From a paper prepared for this biography by Ewart Walters, journalist, 2006
4. From a paper prepared for this biography by Ewart Walters, journalist, 2006
5. *Daily Gleaner*, April 6, 1967
6. *Daily Gleaner*, April 7, 1967
7. *Daily Gleaner*, April 4, 1967
8. *Daily Gleaner*, April 4, 1967
9. *Daily Gleaner*, April 4, 1967
10. *Daily Gleaner*, April 5, 1967
11. Interview with Ambassador Peter King, former personal assistant to Robert Lightbourne
12. *Daily Gleaner*, April 5, 1967
13. *Daily Gleaner*, April 5, 1967, p. 12
14. *Daily Gleaner*, April 5, 1967
15. *Daily Gleaner*, April 6, 1967
16. Interview with Hector Wynter, circa 1994
17. *Daily Gleaner*, April 6, 1967
18. *Daily Gleaner*, April 6, 1967
19. *Daily Gleaner*, April 6, 1967
20. *Daily Gleaner*, November 11, 1964
21. *Daily Gleaner*, April 8, 1967
22. An extract from the 1967 autopsy report done in Montreal, Canada, 2002
23. Report by Dr John Stewart of the Montreal Neurological Institute and McGill University, provided to Dr Alfred Sangster, 2002

NB: Every Gleaner publication from March 18 to April 11, 1967, carried an update on the health condition of Donald Sangster

Chapter 28

1. Interview with Clovis McLean, a resident of Mountainside and an early friend of Donald Sangster. "Sammy" who was also interviewed gave a different story. He said Sangster did not catch him
2. Mrs Pauline Mason—now retired, 2006
3. Reminiscing with Gladstone Bonnick, circa 2006
4. Reminiscing with Lance Evans, circa 1992
5. *Daily Gleaner*, June 23, 1956, p. 1
6. *Daily Gleaner*, September 23, 1965
7. *Daily Gleaner*, September 24, 1965
8. *Daily Gleaner*, April 15, 1967, p. 10
9. Recollections by Donald Sangster's son, Anthony, 2011

Chapter 29

1. *Daily Gleaner*, April 12, 1967
2. *Daily Gleaner*, April 12, 1967, p. 14
3. *Daily Gleaner*, April 9, 1967, p. 2
4. *Daily Gleaner*, April 12, 1967
5. *Daily Gleaner*, April 14, 1967
6. *Daily Gleaner*, April 15, 1967
7. *Daily Gleaner*, April 16, 1967

Chapter 30

1. *Daily Gleaner*, April 19, 1967
2. *Daily Gleaner*, April 19, 1967
3. A copy of this recording is in the personal files of Alicia Sangster
4. Interview with Dr Alfred Sangster, 2006

©Gary Neita

ABOUT THE AUTHOR HARTLEY NEITA

Hartley Neita started his career in journalism at the age of 17 as a columnist for the Gleaner Company. His colleagues had cheered him as he left his earlier job at the Ministry of Agriculture, for they knew full-well his passion for the power of the written word. His early writings were encouraged by four persons, T.E. Sealy, Vic Reid, Roy Coverley and Joe Lewis.

In 1956 he joined the staff of the newly-formed Government Public Relations Office, the precursor to the Jamaica Information Service. As his career evolved, he served in the unique capacity as press officer and press secretary to five different heads of government for both major political parties in Jamaica:

Press Officer, Norman Manley, 1958 to 1962

Press Secretary, Sir Alexander Bustamante, 1962 to 1965

Press Secretary, Hon. Donald Sangster, 1965 to 1967

Press Secretary, Rt. Hon. Hugh Shearer, 1967 to 1972

Press Secretary, Rt. Hon. Michael Manley, 1989 to 1992

Prior to his death in 2008, Neita authored this biography, *Jamaica's Forgotten Prime Minister—Donald Sangster,* to ensure that the legacy of our second prime minister, a stalwart political figure in Jamaican history, lives on. The working title of his first manuscript made reference to Sangster's contribution to the Commonwealth of Nations. As an active witness to the birth of our nation, Neita takes you behind the scenes of the Jamaican political landscape with an unbiased viewpoint.

Neita is also the author of the quintessential biography of the third prime minsiter of Jamaica, *Hugh Shearer—A Voice for the People*, and the riveting story, *The Search,* which details a true story of five schoolboys lost in the Blue Mountains. Like his two biographies, this latter book paints a picture of a Jamaica seen through his keen eyes, recorded by his sharp memory and penned in his unique style. Hartley Neita's various short stories, newspaper articles, columns and memoirs contributed and commissioned over his 60- year career come from a position of truth and integrity.

www.hartleyneitabooks.com

www.ingramcontent.com/pod-product-compliance
Lightning Source LLC
Chambersburg PA
CBHW030935150426
42812CB00064B/2905/J